BUYING AND SELLING
A SMALL BUSINESS

Michael M. Coltman

Self-Counsel Press
(a division of)
International Self-Counsel Press Ltd.
Vancouver
Toronto   Seattle

Printed in Canada

First edition: October, 1983
Reprinted: May, 1985; September, 1986
Second edition: February, 1989

Canadian Cataloguing in Publication Data
Coltman, Michael M. (Michael Macdonald), 1930-
    Buying and selling a small business

    (Self-counsel series)
    ISBN 0-88908-694-X

    1. Small business — Management. 2. Small busi-
ness — Purchasing. 3. Small business — Valuation.
I. Title. II. Series.
HD62.7.C64 1989   658.1'141   C89-091038-3

Self-Counsel Press
(a division of)
International Self-Counsel Press Ltd.
1481 Charlotte Road
North Vancouver, British Columbia V7J 1H1

CONTENTS

PREFACE

This book is about buying and selling an existing small business. It is written primarily from the perspective of the purchaser, but it is for the seller as well. For every buyer there must be a seller.

As a seller reading this book, you will become more aware of what a prospective purchaser of your business is looking for. That should make you much more alert and aware as a seller. If a prospective purchaser has not read this book, you can provide him or her with the pertinent information that might persuade that prospective purchaser to become an actual one.

For example you could:

- Point out the advantages of buying an existing business rather than starting a new one from scratch (chapter 2)
- Emphasize the value of your particular location or site (chapter 6)
- Evaluate your own business to present it in a better light (chapter 7)
- Help the purchaser put together financial information about your business to help in financing (chapter 9)
- Guide the buyer to sources of financing that you are familiar with and that will help the purchaser make arrangements for buying (chapters 10, 11, 12)

Certain chapters will be specifically useful to you as seller since selling is simply the reverse of buying.

For example, chapter 8 on valuation methods will explain to you how to establish a reasonable selling price for your business.

The contract details spelled out in chapter 13 are vitally important to you as seller, and you might want to consider leasing some of your assets (chapter 14), rather than selling them, to the purchaser.

Finally, chapters 16 and 17 are specifically written from the seller's point of view.

1

BEFORE YOU BUY A BUSINESS

Entrepreneurship, or going into business for yourself, has become more popular in recent years. Educators, politicians, and even some large business managers are extolling the virtues of entrepreneurship. Entrepreneurship seems to have surfaced recently as the best way to create jobs and help form a more healthy economy.

a. ENTREPRENEURSHIP

The concept of small business entrepreneurship has not always been popular, particularly among young people whom the colleges and universities began training in unprecedented numbers in the '50s and '60s. These graduates were trained in management skills, but these skills were very much oriented to the larger businesses. Indeed, management skills were often specialized for particular industries and businesses.

These large businesses offered good pay, fringe benefits, apparent security over the long term, and eventual retirement pensions. These attractions turned employees away from initiative and entrepreneurship. This trend now seems to be coming to an end with the re-emergence of small business as a possible answer to many economic problems.

1. Survival of small business

Entrepreneurship and small business are not new to this country. Several hundred years ago the small business operator thrived in this country in the form of fur trappers who traded with larger companies (the monopolists of their day). Not much has changed. Today large companies still tend to monopolize many markets, but small business nevertheless continues to thrive and grow by filling a niche that the large companies cannot handle.

Large companies are often the target of strikes, which lead to an inability to serve their customers. They are also subject to distribution problems, unlike many small firms who service a local need.

In addition, more automation of large businesses might lead to fewer jobs. Employees who are no longer required by large firms might adapt well to smaller businesses catering to individual tastes or demands for one-of-a-kind products.

Also, reduced flexibility of large businesses may lead to fewer choices for consumers and thus a need for small businesses to step in and fill that gap.

All this does not mean that there will be a mass return to the cottage industry; but as large firms reduce their labor force and ability to vary products, small firms will move in and pick up the slack. This does not imply that a small firm should take on the giants and expect to succeed. The name of the game is not competition but alternatives.

b. SMALL BUSINESS DEFINITION

What is a small business? Definitions abound — many of them rather meaningless, particularly when expressed in annual sales dollars or number of persons employed. Perhaps the best definition is this: a small business is independently owned and operated and not dominant in its field.

Most small companies are established to manufacture, distribute, and retail a variety of goods and services. Despite the fact that the large corporations receive much press and publicity, most large companies are dependent on small business. For example, companies that mass produce manufactured goods could not possibly distribute them without the myriad of small firms that handle transportation, wholesaling, and retailing for them. In other words, small business enterprises are the backbone of free enterprise economies.

c. SKILLS REQUIRED

If you are going to purchase a small business and have not previously owned or managed a small firm, you need to make sure you have the necessary skills.

Traditionally, the level of management skills has been considerably less in small businesses than in larger ones, but the market that small businesses face is just as complex as the one faced by large corporations.

The management skills required of the small business entrepreneur are basically the same as those of managers in a large business. All managers must plan, make decisions based on the best information available, and prepare strategies for the future.

The small business owner/manager must constantly make decisions that will solve problems, resolve priorities, determine policies, settle financial issues, and so on. In addition, operating results must be analyzed constantly, and outside factors that may have an effect on the internal operations of the business must be considered.

1. Broad responsibilities

The individual small business owner must assume an even wider range of responsibilities than the general manager of a large corporation. The manager of a large corporation will have vice presidents for finance, for marketing, for manufacturing and production, for distribution, and so on. Each of these vice presidents has important responsibilities, but each is concerned with only one specific area of the total company activities.

In the small business, the owner generally has a daily responsibility not only for all of the above but also for ongoing problems concerning personnel, inventory, sales, credit, suppliers, new policy implementation, new product introductions, public relations, marketing, and financial reporting.

d. RISK INVOLVED

If you are entering the small business field for the first time, you also need to know about the risks involved.

Those who go into small business do so in spite of, or in ignorance of, the odds of survival. A rule of thumb for new small businesses is that as many as 50% will fail during the first year and as many as 90% in less than five years.

Statistical analysis of business failures shows that 95% of all business failures are caused by the owner's lack of competence and managerial experience in that particular field.

1. Sizeable investment

Purchasing your own business requires a sizeable investment, not only in money, but also in your time, effort, and energy. If the business is not successful, you may be able to afford the loss. You may also be able to sell the business's assets, such as land and buildings, for more than you paid for them. But that gain will be offset by losses on the sale of equipment and fixtures, inventory, and similar assets that seldom, if ever, repay their original cost. If you do not own the land and a building, you will not have a capital gain to help offset those losses.

Therefore, do not rush into buying a business. In each case, consider the possibility of failure and weigh it in your final decision.

e. PROFESSIONAL HELP

In most situations, you are going to need some professional help with your business purchase.

1. Your banker

For most small businesses, a small local bank branch manager is likely to be of more help than a big city banker who handles only large accounts.

You should advise your banker of your intention to buy a business and keep him or her informed as you make progress in this regard.

Your banker will be able to provide you with useful information about the type of business you decide to buy. For example, if you settle on a retail business of a particular type, your banker probably handles the accounts of other similar retail businesses and can help you evaluate the financial aspects of the business you propose buying.

2. Your accountant

If you do not have accounting experience, you will need an accountant, at least to handle your annual tax return. Tax law and tax accounting for business can be quite complex. Few small business owners have the competence, or the time, to be knowledgeable about all the intricacies of income tax.

This does not mean that you should not try to familiarize yourself with income tax rules and regulations, since that knowledge can be helpful in the day-to-day operation of any business that you buy, but a professional advisor in this area is well worth the cost.

Once you have selected your accountant and banker, you should introduce them to each other. There are going to be several situations that arise in areas such as financing and tax planning where the two of them will need to consult.

3. Your lawyer

Finally, you will probably need a lawyer since the purchase of a business involves some legal matters.

It might be a good idea to have your lawyer and accountant get together, since some of their areas of concern can overlap, and you do not want to pay twice for the same advice.

4. Choosing your professional advisors

To select professional advisors you should shop around. Bankers, accountants, and lawyers, just like any business people, are in competition with each other.

Also, even though these professionals (particularly accountants and lawyers) are members of professional associations and are required to be competent in their field, there are degrees of competence and also degrees of specialization. Do not choose the first one you visit because of a positive first impression, even though that first impression can be important in your final decision.

Tell each professional that you are discussing the situation with two or three others in that profession. They may decide not to charge you for a short initial meeting, since this may encourage you to stay with them in the long run.

Check with friends who are in business, or even with people you meet socially or on other business matters, about professionals they could recommend.

However, do not choose a professional advisor solely because you know him or her socially. Try, in fact, to find a lawyer or accountant who is familiar with the type of business you propose to purchase if you already have some idea of the type of business you would like to buy.

If you plan to locate in a particular area, then selecting a lawyer and an accountant (as well as a banker) in that area is preferable since they will be familiar with local conditions and will be easier to visit when necessary.

5. Be prepared for questions

Professional advisors are going to ask you questions from the outset. You should try to have the answers to these questions ready, even in an exploratory first meeting.

These questions (many of which will be discussed in detail in later chapters) will cover such matters as the type and size of business you are thinking of buying, the organizational form of your company (proprietorship, partnership, or private limited company), the amount of money you can invest yourself, the amount of money you may have to borrow, and the date you plan to take over the business.

6. Cost of professionals

You will want to know how much you are going to pay for professional advice.

Bankers do not normally charge for their time. Their profit is made from the interest they charge for money that you borrow from them and for the use they can make of any business funds you have on deposit with them.

Accountants and lawyers usually charge on an hourly basis, or they may charge an annual retainer fee for certain ongoing day-to-day advice, with an extra charge for matters that fall outside what is included in the retainer. Unless the business you plan to buy is reasonably large and is going to require a great deal of professional advice, your costs will be lower if you do not pay a retainer.

If your accountant is also going to produce your monthly accounts, there will likely be a flat monthly charge for doing this. Filing the annual tax return might be included in this monthly charge. Alternatively, that may be an additional annual cost.

Since accountants and lawyers do have a fairly high hourly fee, you should try to limit the amount of time you use them. As much as possible make decisions for yourself and only call on them when a matter to be resolved is critical and where proper professional help is required.

Also, check at the outset what the procedure is for getting advice. Generally accountants and lawyers, like most business people, prefer to arrange face-to-face meetings with as much advance notice as possible. Finally, they generally prefer not to give advice over the telephone concerning important matters that require documentation.

2

STARTING A BUSINESS
VERSUS BUYING

For the seller: *This chapter points out the advantages of buying an existing business rather than starting a new one from scratch. As a seller, you might want to specifically refer potential purchasers to these advantages.*

You have two major ways of going into business for yourself. One is to start a business from scratch. The other is to buy an existing business. Even though this book is about buying an existing business it might be useful for you to be aware of the pros and cons of starting up a new business — even if all this does is confirm in your own mind that buying an existing business is preferable.

a. STARTING A NEW BUSINESS

1. Advantages

Some of the major advantages of starting a new business are as follows:

- You can select a location that can take advantage of current economic or market conditions.
- If the plans include constructing a new building, the building can be designed to your specifications and the type of business you plan to have.
- The type and size of building can also be designed to conditions as they exist today.
- The building can be constructed of modern materials and have modern equipment and fixtures that are designed to keep maintenance costs to a minimum. Similarly, the design can encompass methods of labor efficiency (in such areas as maintenance) to reduce overall operating costs.
- The design can include a capacity for future additions to the building.

- Expensive future alterations or additions can be anticipated by conforming to existing zoning bylaws and preparing for zoning bylaw changes that could occur.
- The increasing costs of energy can be compensated for by using the most up-to-date energy saving design ideas and materials.

Of course, if you start a new business in an existing building, many of the advantages listed above may not be available to you.

2. Disadvantages

Some of the disadvantages of starting your own business are as follows:

- The time required to put together a financing arrangement to buy the necessary land and put together a building package can be quite long and the financing itself fairly complex.
- The construction and start up time delay caused by putting together a financing package also delays a return on your own investment, and during this time interest will have to be paid on any borrowed money.
- A clientele will have to be built up. This takes time — from a few months in some businesses to two or three years in others. Starting a new business does not, by itself, create an immediate brand new clientele or market.
- A new business, designed and located on a foundation of future demand for its products and/or services may not immediately produce a sufficient return on your investment. In such cases you may find that you have to keep advancing the company new cash to keep it in operation.
- Any new business suffers an additional risk since it will probably have to compete with already existing competitive businesses whose sites and/or locations are more favorable and whose market is already successfully established.
- A new business has many unforeseen hazards to overcome between breaking ground and opening

doors. These hazards include strikes, poor weather, building material shipping delays, and others. This can seriously affect the final cost of construction.

However, note again that some of these disadvantages disappear if you are simply going to start a new business in already existing premises.

b. BUYING AN EXISTING BUSINESS

An alternative to starting a new business is to buy an existing one. Some of the advantages and disadvantages of buying an already existing business operation follow.

1. Advantages

- It is a speedier way of getting into business and eliminates the time, cost, and energy required to plan a new business from scratch.
- You can physically examine the property (building and equipment) you are thinking of purchasing and assess its value.
- You are buying an operating business where financial statements showing actual revenue and expenses can be examined.
- With an already existing business, and past financial statements, you can more readily assess the future potential of the business and reduce the uncertainty.
- If the business being purchased has a good reputation and goodwill (that is, a well-established clientele), and if you maintain the operating standards, an immediate cash flow and a sound return on the investment can be virtually guaranteed.
- In the case of a wholesale or retail business, suppliers are already established.
- A business that is well established because it has a good location has a great advantage over any new business built that does not have a choice of a good location.
- Buying an existing business will probably reduce the financing complexities inherent in putting a brand

new property together. The delays in obtaining a return on investment because of the time required for construction are also avoided.

- Financing may be easier to obtain because you can use already existing assets (land, building, equipment, a lease contract) for collateral, and requests for financing are not based on overly optimistic forecasts of sales but on proven sales of the present owner.

- A business that is for sale has a definite end price. Financing is restricted to a single purchase transaction. This end price will not increase once an agreement has been signed, except perhaps for legal fees and similar closing adjustments.

- You are buying a business operating system that is already established and that you may not need to change.

- Experienced employees who stay with the company are immediately available.

- Since there are often many businesses for sale at any one time there is the possibility of buying a "bargain" business.

- There is also the possibility of picking up a run down business at an extremely low price that, under good management, can eventually be very successful.

2. Disadvantages

Some of the disadvantages of buying an existing business are as follows:

- You have to live with the present location and physical design of the business purchased. Alterations to the structure may be difficult and costly, and additions for expansion of the business may not be possible.

- The present location may have been selected for a market that was good at that time but is now much less desirable.

- You inherit any ill will that the business has.

- You are also temporarily locked in to the pricing structure and other operating policies of the seller. They may be difficult to change.

11

- Lines of merchandise are already established and may not be quite what you want.

- In some cases, you inherit the previous owner's employees who may not be an asset or who may resent you as a new owner.

- You also inherit the customers, making it more difficult to change the company's image.

- If the seller has run down the property (and you will be buying it rather than leasing it), maintenance expenses to bring it back into shape may be costly. In the same vein, if sales have declined because of such matters as poor maintenance and poor management practices it may take considerable time to build back the declined sales and customer goodwill.

- If the property is older, maintenance costs will be higher than for a new property; if the plumbing and wiring are antiquated, the costs for replacement can be exorbitant. However, if the building is to be leased, these costs would normally be borne by the landlord and simply passed on to you in an increased rental charge.

- You may have to pay for the present owner's "goodwill" (the present value of future business potential due to established customers and business reputation) and the value of this goodwill may be difficult to assess.

- There is a risk, without it being immediately obvious, of buying a poor business or inheriting a lawsuit (for which you may be responsible) that you don't know about.

- There may be changes coming in that business or industry that you are not familiar with since you may not have had previous experience in it.

3. Conclusion

A general conclusion to all of this is that the advantages of taking over an existing business probably outweigh the disadvantages, and that it is generally less risky to do this than to start a new business from scratch.

c. BUYING THE FAILING BUSINESS

It was mentioned that one of the advantages of buying an existing business is that there may be an opportunity to buy a failing business at a relatively low price.

A failing or distressed business can often be found for sale. Given the right circumstances you might end up with a very good return on your investment.

However, follow through on the potential of purchasing a failing business only if you are knowledgeable about the business or industry you are considering.

The cause of the failure should only be from poor management, and not for reasons such as lack of market for the product or service (unless the present market is unable to support the business but has good potential for growth). Alternatively, if the cause for failure is underfinancing of the present business and you have the available capital to put into it, it might be worth investigating.

If the business is already in bankruptcy and under receivership, the decision on the selling price is no longer that of the owner but of the receiver or trustee who may possibly still need the present owner's approval of any offered price.

Any offer that you make to buy such a business must also cover the legal and administrative expenses of the trustee. An initial offer may be rejected by the trustee, but sometimes trustees later reconsider earlier offers since they don't like to manage bankrupt businesses and will opt out if the offer is reasonable.

In all cases of failing or bankrupt businesses, you must be sure of the background of the business. Unless you clearly know what went wrong and know how to correct the problem you might find yourself continuing to run the business as a loser. Any business purchase requires careful investigation (as you will see in chapter 7), but a failing or failed business needs even more rigorous checking.

13

3

GETTING STARTED

You probably want to buy a business for one, or a combination of, the following reasons:
- You want to make a lot of money.
- You want to be your own boss and work when you want to and not when someone else wants you to.
- You have a good idea that you can introduce to society that no one else has ever thought of — or if they have, you can do it better.
- Your talents and/or expertise have not been recognized by those for whom you have worked so far.
- You can only control your own destiny by being independent.
- Satisfaction and/or security and/or the desire for power can only be achieved by running your own business.

a. ELEMENTS REQUIRED

However, in order to be successful in a small business enterprise you have to put together a package that contains most, if not all, of the following elements:

(a) Product, service, or idea that differs from anything on the market or is an improvement over current competitive products, services, or ideas.

(b) Knowledge or experience in following through on that product, service, or idea.

(c) A strategy or marketing plan to help ensure the implementation of your new business.

(d) Appropriate management skills and character.

(e) Financial resources to carry you through critical periods.

Obviously, if you buy an existing business, you have already met some of these requirements (for example items (a), (b), and (c)) since they are in place to a greater or lesser degree.

1. Characteristics for success

Numerous studies have been conducted to determine the characteristics that make a successful small business entrepreneur. There is no one answer about what constitutes the right blend of characteristics, since what is important in one individual may be less important in another, and the type of product or service that you are dealing with can have a bearing.

In general, though, the following characteristics, to a greater or lesser extent, and in some combination, appear to be important:

(a) Drive or energy and the willingness to take responsibility, take risks, make decisions, and accept the consequences

(b) Personal initiative and the ability to get the ball rolling rather than rely on others or defer decisions to others or to committees

(c) Personality and human relations ability: this includes matters such as emotional stability, sociability, cheerfulness in adversity, cooperation, tact, and consideration for others

(d) Organizational ability with an eye to detail so that those around you don't have to guess what needs to be done and who has to do it

(e) Communication ability, both written and oral: you have to be able to communicate with employees, suppliers, customers, bankers, and all the other people you deal with daily

(f) Administrative ability in planning, setting goals and objectives, deciding how to measure results, controlling the business, interpreting financial statements, and similar matters

(g) Technical knowledge about the business: this means not only knowing what you do know but also where you may be deficient in certain skills and technical abilities so that you can upgrade yourself or hire employees competent in that area

(h) Good judgment, patience, and restraint

(i) Leadership

Looking over that list, you might think that only a god could survive in the business world. However, this is only a list of desirable characteristics that are helpful in most situations; lacking one or several of them is not necessarily indicative of failure.

2. Willingness for hard work

There is one characteristic that is generally absolutely essential and that is the willingness to work hard. Without that, in a small business, you are almost certainly doomed to failure since you have the sole responsibility for the ultimate success or failure of your business.

If you do work hard, you should achieve success. That success will be measured not only in having a profitable firm, but also in the rewards that are less easy to measure, such as being satisfied with your working environment, being your own boss, having pride in company ownership, enjoying status in the community, and owning an outlet for creative ideas.

b. SELF TEST

Before you embark on a business venture of your own, it might be a good idea to try the following self test of 10 simple questions. After each question check the answer that describes how you feel, or comes closest to it. It is important to be honest with yourself.

16

SELF-TEST FOR BUSINESS SUCCESS

1. How do you react to other people?
   - ☐ a. I like people and get along with almost everybody.
   - ☐ b. I have lots of friends and don't need any more.
   - ☐ c. Other people annoy me.

2. Are you a self motivator?
   - ☐ a. I start things myself and I don't need others to get me motivated.
   - ☐ b. Sometimes I need others to get me going.
   - ☐ c. Why should I put myself out until I have to?

3. What about leadership potential?
   - ☐ a. When I begin something most people seem to go along with it.
   - ☐ b. I'm all right as long as someone gives me some direction.
   - ☐ c. Once someone gets things going I'll cooperate as long as I agree with it.

4. Are you a good organizer?
   - ☐ a. I like to plan ahead; even if someone comes up with a good idea I'm usually the one to map out a plan.
   - ☐ b. Planning isn't that necessary; as long as things work out I feel O.K.
   - ☐ c. What's the point in planning — someone will just come along and mess it up.

5. Can you handle responsibility?
   - ☐ a. I'm a take charge person. Someone has to take control and see things through.
   - ☐ b. If nobody else will take charge I don't mind accepting the responsibility.
   - ☐ c. Why should I bother when I can leave it to those who want to show how smart they are at assuming control?

6. Do you like work?

☐ a. If it's something I want I'll work as long and as hard as necessary.

☐ b. I find I can only work so much at a task before bowing out.

☐ c. Hard work is for fools.

7. What about perseverance?

☐ a. Nothing stops me once I've decided a goal is worthwhile.

☐ b. As long as it doesn't get messed up by someone else I'll finish what I start.

☐ c. If I see things might not work out I quit. Why fight a losing battle?

8. Are you able to make decisions?

☐ a. I can make decisions and more than 50% of the time I'm correct.

☐ b. I need time to make decisions. I have to talk to everybody involved. Most of the time they give me mixed advice.

☐ c. Why should I always have to make decisions that are other people's responsibility?

9. Are you determined?

☐ a. Once I have decided to go ahead with a project, nothing gets in my way.

☐ b. As long as someone else doesn't get in my way, I can usually finish what I start.

☐ c. If things go right from the beginning, I'll persevere until there is a problem.

10. What about your health?

☐ a. I'm full of energy seven days a week.

☐ b. I'm full of energy for the things I like to do.

☐ c. How come all my friends and acquaintances are so full of energy?

1. Now count up your score

a. Number of check marks beside the first answer to each question: _____

b. Number of check marks beside the second answer to each question: _____

c. Number of check marks beside the third answer to each question: _____

If most of your check marks are beside the first answers, you probably have the right qualities to run your own business. If not, your chances of success are considerably lessened and you might find it a good idea to work with a partner who is stronger in the areas where you have a weakness.

If most of your checks are alongside the third answer, not even a great partner will be able to prop you up.

On the other hand, a good score on the above test is no guarantee of success; all the other elements of a successful business must be in place to ensure that.

The test is primarily designed to give you an insight into your relative strengths and weaknesses. If you have any weaknesses, you should decide how you are going to overcome them before going too far along the road to purchasing and running your own business.

2. Other questions

In addition to the above questions, you should also face up to the following:

(a) Do you have the mental and physical stamina to run your own business?

(b) Are you prepared to sacrifice your present lifestyle to this new venture?

(c) Are your spouse and family (if any) willing to accept the change and possible upheaval in your lifestyle?

(d) Have you determined how much income you need to survive during this period of change?

(e)   Can you survive if all your income has to come from a new venture that may or may not be successful?

If the answer to each of these five questions is not a definite yes, then it is possible you may be acting on emotion rather than in an objective way. In that case, if you do not succeed, you have only yourself to blame.

c. RETIREMENT AND RUNNING YOUR OWN BUSINESS

If you are retired, or close to it, you may be planning to buy and run your own small business. If that is the case, your probable objectives are to have a relatively trouble free business that will provide you with a secure income and permit you to organize for the future for eventual disposition of the business in your estate planning.

Be cautious. It may not be easy to find a business that will be profitable in the short run. If you have to use pension funds, or cash from an insurance policy to buy into a business, you may be taking a great risk.

Also, if you have been an employee of a larger business throughout your career, you will find the risks and strains of running your own business quite different, and perhaps even impossible to adapt to after 40 or more years of working for an organization where you merely followed policies and procedures decided by others. You may find yourself working six days a week in a retail store, or even seven days a week if you buy a restaurant. Holidays may never materialize unless you can afford to pay for a manager in your absence.

If the business you plan to buy is quite different from the one you previously worked in, you may suddenly find you don't like it. One way to offset that is to take a job, part-time if necessary, in that kind of business to help confirm in your own mind that it is what you want before risking your hard-earned savings or pension funds.

Finally, the decisions you make will be all yours. There may be no one to turn to for help, or to blame if things go wrong.

4

LEGAL FORMS OF ORGANIZATION

Once you have decided to purchase a business, and you are sure you have the right qualities to survive, one of the earliest decisions that you have to make is the legal organizational form that the enterprise will take. The three common types of organization are the proprietorship, the partnership, and the limited company.

a. PROPRIETORSHIP

The easiest way for you to establish an organization with little or no cost or legal problems is to operate a proprietorship. Many businesses are operated this way, with the owner responsible for the actions and liabilities of the business, even if the day-to-day running of it, or parts of it, is delegated to others.

As a proprietorship, you would be financed primarily from your personal savings, from bank loans, sometimes from government loans, and, if the business is successful, from the profits of the business reinvested in it.

The profit of the proprietorship is the personal income of the owner and is taxed, with any salary paid to him or her by the business, at personal tax rates. Any loans from creditors or investors are made to the owner and not the company.

Proprietorships do not issue shares of any kind, as do limited companies (which will be discussed later). Businesses established as proprietorships must still conform to regulatory authorities such as, for example, local licensing authorities in order to obtain a license to legally operate as a business.

1. Advantages

The main advantages of a proprietorship are that as owner you have total control, do not have to consider the opinions of partners or other business associates (thus speeding the decision-making process), and will reap the full financial rewards for your efforts.

There are also minimal legal restrictions with a proprietorship and it can be easily discontinued if and when this might be appropriate.

2. Disadvantages

Some disadvantages are that, theoretically, the organization ceases to exist when the owner dies. The assets of the company become part of the owner's estate and are subject to estate and inheritance taxes, if any. Thus it may be difficult for relatives to continue the business.

A proprietorship may also find it difficult to expand since it does not have the same opportunities to raise capital as do other types of business organizations that have a broader base of financial resources.

Also, generally speaking, in case of bankruptcy or a serious lawsuit you may find that your personal assets (such as your house, car, and personal savings) as well as the company's assets may be seized to satisfy the liabilities of the organization. In other words, the proprietorship's liability is unlimited. This is probably the major disadvantage of a proprietorship.

b. PARTNERSHIP

Unlike the sole proprietorship, the partnership is generally a more formal type of business organization. It is a legal association between two or more individuals or co-owners of a business.

Although a partnership does not require a written agreement, all partners probably should agree to a negotiated contract, or articles of partnership. The terms of these articles will vary widely from one enterprise to another, but they should include at least the name of the company; the name of each partner; the rights, contributions, and benefits of each partner; how the profits and losses are to be distributed (without an agreement to the contrary they are assumed to be distributed equally); and the length of the life of the partnership.

In a partnership, each partner may represent the company and enter into contracts on its behalf. Each partner is also personally liable for the debts of the company incurred by other partners. This personal liability (as is in a proprietorship) is unlimited.

Partnerships are not taxed at the limited company tax rates. Instead, the business's net income, or loss, is shared according to the terms of the partnership contract, and each partner includes that share, plus any salary received from the company, on his or her personal tax return.

Partnerships, like proprietorships, do not issue shares of any kind, and must conform to regulatory authorities.

1. Advantages

The main advantages of partnerships are that they are relatively easy to organize, that financing is sometimes easier to obtain and that (since there is more than one owner), the total partnership investment can be much greater than in a proprietorship. A partnership may also have a greater depth of combined good judgment and managerial skills.

2. Disadvantages

The disadvantages of a partnership are that upon one partner's death or withdrawal from the business (except in the case of a limited partner discussed later), the partnership may have to be dissolved and reorganized. This can make it difficult to continue the company's operations.

It can also create financial difficulties for the business if the dead partner's heirs disagree with the company's evaluation of his or her share of the company. Also, the heirs will have to be bought out, which may impose a financial burden on the remaining partners.

Another disadvantage of the partnership is that since in many cases all partners may need to be consulted, quick decisions about the company's operations may be difficult to make and serious disagreements can occur.

Also, partners are not only responsible for the debts and obligations they have contracted for, but they are also responsible for those contracted by all other partners.

Finally, it may be difficult to remove an incompetent partner or one you don't get along with. Difficulties often arise with partners concerning the direction the business should go and how it should be run. Sometimes considerable interpersonal skills are necessary to overcome these difficulties.

However, these difficulties in themselves can also be opportunities since, in discussing them, mutually agreeable objectives and plans will often materialize. This, in itself, can be an advantage compared to operating as a proprietorship where you may have no one knowledgeable about your business to discuss it with.

To minimize areas of conflict in a partnership you might consider including in the partnership agreement details concerning the following typical questions:

- Who is responsible for various aspects of the business, for example, production and marketing?
- Who establishes operating policies and, indeed, what constitutes a policy? Are policies, or changes of policies, decided by a majority vote of the partners, or by some other method?
- What expenses, for example, car mileage and entertainment expenses, can be charged to the business?

3. Limited partnership

The partnership type of organization discussed above is referred to as a general partnership. Another form of partnership is known as a limited partnership.

A limited partnership has both general partners with unlimited personal liability and limited partners with limited personal liability. The partnership contract should spell out this limited personal liability. It should also

24

indicate the amount that the limited partner(s) have invested.

A limited partnership arrangement is made when limited, or silent, partners wish to invest in a company and obtain a return on their investment without being personally involved in the day-to-day decision-making and operation of the business.

c. LIMITED COMPANY

Many small businesses are organized as limited companies. The limited company, unlike the proprietorship and partnership, is a separate legal entity, with its own rights and duties, that can continue as a separate business even after the death of an owner.

A limited company can be created for any size of business (although some professions do not allow their members to do this). It is wrong to consider it appropriate only for larger companies.

Establishing a limited company is both more complex and more costly (from a legal and accounting point of view) than establishing a proprietorship or a partnership, but it is probably the most effective way of operating a business.

For regulatory purposes, a limited company is like a person. It can sue and be sued, just like an individual, and it must conform to regulatory authorities. A limited company is an ongoing organization with an infinite life of its own even though employees and owners come and go. Many of its assets, such as the land and the building, may indeed have a life longer than the life of the shareholders.

1. Public versus private companies

Limited companies may be established as either public or private. A public company is generally one that has its shares listed on a stock exchange. The legal requirements for operating a public company are much more strict than those for a private company. However, you will more likely be interested in organizing a private limited company since that type of company is designed for the small business operator.

2. Incorporation

You can have a lawyer set up the limited company for you or, in many cases, you can do this for yourself since books are available that show you step by step how this is done. Doing it yourself may save you several hundred dollars. However, if the situation, for one reason or another, is complex, then professional legal advice should be sought. For example, depending on your personal financial situation, there may be advantages to establishing the share structure of the company one way rather than another.

3. Advantages

The major advantage of the limited company form of business is that, generally speaking, since the company is a separate legal entity, the individual owners cannot be held responsible for the company's liabilities. The owners, in other words, have a liability limited to their investment in shares in the company.

However, despite this, lending institutions that you approach for financing will generally make you sign a personal note to extend your liability outside the protection offered by the company. This is particularly true if it is a new business.

Another advantage is that financing may be facilitated by the creation of easily transferable certificates of ownership, known as shares, that may be bought by or sold to others, including employees of the company.

This broadens the base of financing available to the company. The limited liability of share ownership appeals to some investors since it permits ownership, with a potential return on the investment, without involvement in the company's day-to-day operations.

There may also be some personal tax advantages to forming a limited company (rather than a proprietorship or partnership) that make that form of business appealing. Since each individual situation is different you should consult your accountant for the tax pros and cons of forming a limited company.

4. Disadvantages

One disadvantage of forming a limited company is that, depending on its size and number of owners, decision-making can be a lengthy process.

Dilution of control and profits can also occur if there are a great many shareholders (although this would not normally be true of the typical private limited company).

Also, double taxation exists for shareholders of limited companies. The corporation pays taxes on its profit at the corporate tax rate. Any after-tax income may be distributed to the individual shareholders as dividends. The individual is then taxed for these dividends at personal tax rates.

A limited company is subject to more government regulation and form filing than is a proprietorship or a partnership — although this is a small price to pay considering the advantages that incorporation may offer.

5. Subchapter "S"

In the U.S. you do have a tax option known as subchapter "S". A subchapter "S" corporation is a special form of business organization, permitted for tax reporting purposes only, in which the incorporated company, unlike normal incorporated companies, pays no income tax.

Instead, the corporate earnings are taxed in the stockholders' hands as if they were partnership income to those stockholders.

There are rules and restrictions on how a subchapter "S" corporation may be formed. Since these rules and regulations change from time to time you should have your lawyer tell you what they are when you are ready to decide about this option.

Finally, there may be some personal tax advantages to forming a limited company that make it more appealing than subchapter "S". Since each individual situation is different consult your accountant for the tax pros and cons in your particular case.

5

TYPE OF BUSINESS AND PRODUCTS

You may have already decided on the type of business that you want to purchase and the type of products and services it will handle. In that case you might wish to skim this chapter.

a. TYPE OF BUSINESS

Although there is a broad range of types of businesses, most of them can be categorized as one or other of the following: manufacturing, wholesaling, retailing, or service.

1. Manufacturing

Manufacturing companies generally convert raw materials that may have been mined, or even manufactured at a primary level, into products that are used by other manufacturing firms or, if in finished state, sold to wholesalers or consumers.

Manufacturers of consumer items bear the burden of advertising their products to consumers (despite the fact they do not generally sell directly to them) simply because the manufacturer has the biggest investment in the sale of its products.

2. Wholesaling

Many small businesses operate at the wholesale level in industrial and consumer goods. Manufacturers need wholesalers so that they don't have to go into, and incur the costs of, distributing one or a few product lines.

The wholesaler, on the other hand, can handle product lines from several manufacturers, and thus offer the retailer a wide variety of products without the retailer having to deal with a diversity of manufacturers.

A wholesaler does not generally sell to the public and may only have a few customers. Sales are made through sales persons rather than by advertising. Wholesalers are sometimes called distributors.

3. Retailing

Retailing businesses, as well as being the most visible type of business, form the largest percentage of small businesses. They offer a whole host of products and services to the public.

Retailing attracts small business entrepreneurs because of its general ease of entry at relatively low cost compared to manufacturing and, to a lesser degree, wholesaling.

The retailer generally buys from the manufacturer or wholesaler and sells to the ultimate consumer.

There are two basic kinds of retailers. There are those who work on a personal basis with their customers, often with an office in the home. This is often called direct sales. The other type is those who work from a store or shop location.

Both types of retailer must seek or attract customers and, for this reason, sales may be very dependent on advertising.

Some of the more common retailing businesses include:
Appliances
Auto parts and supplies
Bakeries
Building materials
Clothes
Department stores
Drug stores
Electronic appliances
Furniture
Garden equipment and supplies
Gas stations
Groceries
Hardware
Heating and air conditioning
Home furnishings

Jewelry, watches, diamonds
Mail order houses
Medical, surgical, hospital supplies
Mobile homes
New and used cars
Office equipment and supplies
Photographic equipment and supplies
Plumbing and heating
Radios, TVs, music
Restaurants
Roofing and siding
Shoes
Sporting goods
Variety goods
Vending machines

4. Service

Generally service firms are categorized as those that are not directly involved in offering a tangible product that is bought and sold. Although there may be products or parts involved, it is frequently the work skill or the service of the business's employees that the customer is primarily paying for.

A list of the more common service businesses would include:

Accountants
Athletic clubs
Auto parking
Auto and auto body repair
Bowling alleys
Car rental and leasing
Consulting and public relations
Coin operated laundries
Computer and data processing services
Dance schools
Dental laboratories
Drive-in theatres
Equipment rental and leasing

Funeral services
Hotels and motels
Insurance
Legal firms
Motion picture theatres
Outdoor advertising
Photo studios
Radio and TV repair
Real estate

b. PRODUCT TYPES

There are two major types of products: industrial and retail.

1. Industrial products

Industrial products are goods sold to other businesses for use in products that they manufacture, or for their own consumption (for example, cleaning supplies). Industrial products include raw materials, partly manufactured goods, manufactured goods that become parts of other products, equipment and machinery, and supplies of many kinds.

A small firm selling to industrial product users is in some ways in a more competitive market since the product buyers are generally better informed about the products they buy than the end consumer is. In other words, product performance is more important than the emotional appeal of an advertisement.

Industrial products are also generally more sensitive to changing market conditions that affect prices. They frequently require the seller to produce to the purchaser's specifications.

Since there are relatively fewer purchasers of industrial products than there are purchasers at the retail level, the average sale is invariably higher but, at the same time, the seller is more apt to be affected by changed demand.

Since intermediaries are seldom used for industrial goods, the producer or manufacturer is required to make direct contact with potential buyers and be familiar with who they might be. In other words, the market conditions for the producer and seller of industrial products are quite different from the market for the sale of retail products.

A retailer probably would not normally handle any industrial products, but a manufacturer or wholesaler might well be dealing with retail products.

2. Retail products

Retail, or consumer, products have their own particular characteristics that require different merchandising skills depending on the type of product you are dealing with. Retail, or consumer, products can generally be classified as convenience products, shopping products, or specialty products.

(a) Convenience products

Convenience products are items that the consumer wishes to buy with the minimum of effort where price is not an important consideration.

Convenience food stores are typical of an outlet for convenience products. They offer staple items of relatively low value that customers want as quickly as possible and that they may not be able to buy anywhere else at the time the items are needed.

The merchandising of convenience products generally does not require highly qualified sales personnel. Proximity to competitors is not a problem since such stores often are open when others are closed.

The variety of product lines they carry is limited to the most likely items that customers will want in an emergency. The layout of convenience stores is important since the profit realized from sale of impulse items can be considerable.

(b) Shopping products

Shopping products are those for which purchasers shop around before buying. Consumers compare prices, quality, fashion, level of service, and similar factors. Shopping products are not purchased as frequently as convenience products since their prices are relatively higher.

Most household goods, clothing, and cars are examples of products for which the customer generally will spend a considerable time making comparisons before deciding to purchase.

For these types of products fairly knowledgeable sales personnel are required, and they should be paid accordingly since their ability to explain the advantages of your products over competitive lines is important and their ability to influence customers in determining value for money is essential.

Surprisingly, retail stores selling shopping products of similar types are often found close to each other since this provides the customers a convenient method of shopping around and making comparisons.

(c) Specialty products

Specialty products are invariably of relatively high value, but this high value is not a major concern to prospective purchasers who are more concerned with quality, or at least perceived quality. Examples are jewelry and high class clothing.

Purchasers will not be deterred from seeking out the shop that carries the product brand they want.

Attractiveness of the store and high levels of service are more important here than for convenience or shopping products. Discount price sales are not a major consideration but advertising can be more widespread since prospective purchasers will travel further to buy the brand they desire.

Not all retail products fall neatly into one of the three broad categories outlined. There is a lot of overlap to products, and even of customers. What one customer considers a convenience item another might consider a shopping product. What is important to you, as a potential product retailer, is knowing your market and how its customers perceive your products.

3. Characteristics for product survival

However, regardless of the business you eventually choose to buy, and regardless of whether it is to handle industrial or retail products, there are some general characteristics that seem to determine which products will survive in the marketplace. These characteristics tend to suggest that a product will survive if it has the following characteristics.

(a) It has a relatively large market and there is no dominant supplier (that is, it is not a monopolistic situation).

(b) It is similar to other products that have survived and is as acceptable as those other products.

(c) It is easily recognizable.

(d) It has one or more advantages (such as appearance, packaging, price, or performance) over its competitors.

(e) It can be upgraded to keep it competitive if the need arises, or abandoned when its life cycle is over.

c. WHICH PARTICULAR BUSINESS?

Given the wide variety of types of business and products they sell, which one should the entrepreneur select?

Obviously, you should select a growth industry or business in preference to any other. However, how do you find out which are the growth industries? That's a more difficult question to answer since a growth industry this year may be a declining industry next year due to changing technology, or changing consumer demands. For example, the very successful Swiss watch industry was badly hurt when it began to face competition from the manufacturers of electronic watches.

1. Helpful organizations

The following organizations, among others, can frequently offer valuable information and advice concerning expected growth rates in various industries:

(a) Banks and similar financial institutions, particularly if they have business development departments separate from their normal banking activities)

(b) Various government departments of industry, trade and commerce

(c) Venture capital companies (more about these in a later chapter on financing)

These organizations can also be very helpful to you in other ways, as can government departments involved in small business development.

You should also consult your local trade associations, Chamber of Commerce, and libraries (both general and university/college ones), particularly if they have business sections.

Throughout this book, where appropriate, reference will be made to these and other sources of useful information and aid.

2. Compatibility with goals

It is also important to be aware of the working hours and requirements of any business that you are contemplating buying. You need to seek out a business that is compatible with your ideals and goals, as well as your lifestyle.

For example, if you do not like working 12 or more hours a day, seven days a week, then you should probably stay away from the restaurant business.

You must also decide if you want to run the business directly yourself or buy one that is large enough for "absentee" ownership where you can hire a manager to run it.

3. Funding required

Finally, you must, even at this early stage, have some idea of the amount of money you have available or wish to invest. Financing will be covered in some depth in later chapters, but if you only have, let us say, $50,000 of cash that you can put into a business, it might be unwise to raise your sights too high investigating a business that requires a total investment of $1,000,000.

Regardless of outside cash that you may be able to raise, it is a general rule of thumb that you will have to put in at least 10% of the required cash and perhaps as much as 25%. Therefore, if you only have $50,000 cash, you should be looking for a business whose total purchase cost is in the $200,000 to $500,000 range.

d. SEEKING OPPORTUNITIES

If you do decide in favor of buying an existing business, you must seek out opportunities that meet your ambitions and cash availability. Some ways to do this are:

(a) Newspaper classified advertisements, particularly those in the business opportunities section.

(b) Real estate brokers who specialize in business opportunities. In particular search out those who can both find and screen businesses and who will ensure that all proper legal steps are taken. However, realtors or business brokers receive a commission from the seller that may cause the price to the buyer to increase. This commission is often a percentage of the ultimate selling price.

(c) Trade journals specializing in advertising businesses of the type you are looking for

(d) Word-of-mouth from contacts you have in the type of business you are looking for

(e) Your local Chamber of Commerce or Board of Trade is familiar with many businesses in the local area and may even know of business owners interested in selling their businesses. They may also provide leads (through their counterparts in other towns or cities) if you are looking for business opportunities outside your own community.

(f) Trade sources of the type of business you are looking for can be an excellent information bank. These trade sources include the suppliers, manufacturers, distributors, and trade associations.

(g) Accountants, business consultants, and lawyers all work with small business owners and are often aware of businesses that are for sale. If you don't have an accountant or a lawyer already, you are going to need their services. In your selection of these professionals you can sound them out about their awareness of available businesses.

(h) Your local bank manager may be of help. Businesses need financing. Much of this may be bank financing. Your own bank manager, through information from other branches, may be aware of businesses that have been financed that are for sale.

(i) Finally, don't overlook the business owner! If you have sized up a specific business, you may find, on approaching the owner, that he or she had not even thought about selling. A little persuasion on your part may be all that is needed. Many businesses are sold by this most direct form of contact. Every business is for sale at some price.

6

FINDING A SITE

For the seller: *This chapter shows you how to emphasize the value of your location or site.*

Once you have settled on the type of business you wish to have, and the product(s) and service(s) it will handle, you then need to seek out businesses of that type that are well sited.

In this chapter, it is assumed that the general location of your business has been selected. Location, in this sense, means you have made a decision about the community or area in which you wish to do business and that you are now down to the choice of a specific site within that location.

a. RUNNING A BUSINESS FROM YOUR HOME

Certain types of small businesses may be appropriate to operate out of your home. This is particularly true for some service businesses such as accounting or consulting firms. However, it can also be appropriate for a mail order or light distributing or wholesale business in the early stages of its growth.

Operating a small business out of your residence is not much different from operating out of an office, a shop, or a warehouse, and does offer the following advantages:

(a) You avoid traffic problems and save money by reducing your traveling time.

(b) As well as being allowed to deduct expenses that relate specifically to the business part of your home (for example, plants and pictures) you can claim a portion of your general home expenses (depreciation, mortgage interest, maintenance, property taxes, and insurance) as a business expense.

Since what you can deduct depends on the individual circumstances you should consult your tax accountant about this, particularly with reference to the pros and cons of claiming part of the building depreciation as a business deduction. Remember, however, that if you do buy a business that you can operate from your home you will still probably need a business license.

b. IMPORTANCE OF SITE

If you do not plan to buy a business that you can operate from home, site selection can be critical.

Obviously, in most cases where you are buying an existing business, the site has already been well chosen by the present owner, or his or her predecessor. Nevertheless, it is important for you to understand the factors that create a good site since what might have originally been a good site for the business may no longer be so.

Sites are often selected because of their proximity to where the busines owner lives or because the premise happens to be vacant. Don't fall into this trap unless you have subjected the site to some suitability tests.

Statements made about suitable sites are frequently accompanied by rules of thumb. Beware of rules of thumb. For example, one rule of thumb in a motel site situation is that it should be on the right hand side of the road. This is fine if the motel is to attract potential customers as they approach a community that they are planning to stay in overnight.

But many travelers prefer to drive through a community and stay on its far side overnight so that they can more quickly continue their trip the next day. To such customers a convenient motel on the right (as they exit the center of the community) is on the left for those approaching from the other direction.

Perhaps a more practical general rule of thumb is to select a site that suits the needs of the customers who are the market for the business. You should become familiar with the specifics of the business you are interested in to understand its particular site and market requirements.

1. Site specialist

If you are unfamiliar with the market requirements of a particular business, you may want to approach a site specialist. The services of site selection companies include analysis of population density, customer profiles, access and traffic flows, the drawing power of other businesses in the area, visibility of business and signs, the average sale you should have per square foot, and what effect any nearby competitors or new ones will have. Note, though, that assessing a commercial site is both complex and tricky. It is more art than science, and even the specialists can be wrong.

Even though you may rely on a site specialist to help with site selection, there are some obvious things that you should be aware of. For example, you would not want to locate in an area populated or frequented by people of a different socio-economic base than you must sell your product or service to.

Similarly, you wouldn't want to have a particular type of restaurant in an area that is populated with people whose ethnic background is not oriented to the type of food you will be selling. Nor would you want to locate a business geared to selling to the younger generation in an area inhabited by older married couples.

A good retail site is frequently one near another store that is successfully attracting the kind of people you need as a market base. Sometimes a difference of 20 or 30 feet in site can have a drastic impact, one way or another, on sales.

This is particularly true of shopping center or shopping mall sites. For example, if you are selling impulse items in a shopping mall, a site close to the main traffic flow at the entrance to a major department store, or by an escalator, would be better than at the end of a corridor that, comparatively, is never busy.

c. VISIBILITY, ACCESSIBILITY, AND SUITABILITY

Three extremely important aspects of a good site are visibility, accessibility, and suitability. Each of these will be briefly discussed.

1. Visibility

Visibility of the business may be more important to the customer who arrives at your front door by automobile than it is for the pedestrian, but even for the pedestrian visibility is still important.

Poor visibility of a business outlet can be improved by appropriate outdoor advertising signs that can both attract attention and give directions. This is especially true in a site where the business might be surrounded by larger and taller buildings and where such problems as one way streets and other complications can confuse the customer traveling by car.

2. Accessibility

A second factor in site location is accessibility, again particularly for those arriving by automobile. An ideal situation is where traffic flow in and around the site minimizes the effects of such things as left turn restrictions that prevent the motorist from easily approaching the business.

Equally important is a knowledge about future street and highway changes that could change a desirable access into an undesirable one.

If a routing from the main travel stream is difficult and sign ordinances prohibit providing the motorist with information such as where to turn to reach the business, an infinitely large number of potential customers may be lost.

3. Suitability

Even for a site with good visibility and easy access a critical factor is the suitability of the site. For many businesses, such as a restaurant, a motel, or a building supply outlet the greatest site limitation is space for parking. The space required for parking is usually greater than that required for the building.

Is the site suitable for building expansion? For example, is it reasonably flat and free of rock outcroppings that might be expensive to remove or build around? Is road frontage adequate? Is there sufficient soil depth for the building so that large quantities of fill are not required? Even if your investment cash does not allow buying more land than is immediately needed, it might be a good idea to select a site with adjacent land that could, in the future, be available to buy for building expansion.

d. BYLAWS AND SIMILAR PROBLEMS

Before going too far with buying a business on what seems a desirable site it is best to make sure that all the local bylaws such as zoning restrictions, building codes, fire regulations, and similar laws will allow you to expand the premises once you take over.

For example, if zoning does not allow a larger building on the site, or if there are such problems as height restrictions, can a change in zoning (a variance) be obtained from the local government?

Sign ordinances should also be checked to determine if there are any restrictions on type, placement, number, and size of signs. Make sure that the information obtained concerning bylaws and ordinances is up to date since changes do occur in these regulations from time to time.

A check with the local engineering or public works department will provide information about the suitability of sewers, water mains, and electrical power supplies. If these are not adequate for the size of building planned, the cost to upgrade them could be prohibitive.

The proximity of connection points for utility services is also important since the cost for extra hookups to one or more of these services that might be several hundred yards away could be exorbitant.

The highways department should be approached to provide information concerning future plans for new highways and/or bypass routes that could severely affect the visibility and accessibility of the business. For example, if the business is on a two lane highway that is slated for widening to four lanes, will a divider separate the two halves of the highway? If this is the case it may make it difficult, if not impossible, for arriving or departing motorists to drive directly into or out of the property.

The land deed should be checked to see what easements or other restrictions there are. Are there any buildings on the land that will first have to be demolished? If so this cost of demolition must be added to the asking price for the land.

1. Property appraisal

Before making the final commitment to purchase a business including its building or building and land, an appraisal is recommended. This appraisal will allow comparison of the site selected with information about similar properties in the area. If necessary, obtain a second appraisal for confirmation. The money invested in this will ensure that the business is not located on an overpriced, unsuitable site.

e. LOCATION FACTORS

Some specific questions that you might like to have the answers to for general types of business are as follows.

1. Manufacturing

(a) Is it in a general industrial area that is appropriately zoned?

(b) Is it near a major market or center of several markets?

(c) Is it close to a supply of raw materials? (This is preferable in most cases.)

(d) Are the facilities making the best possible use of production layout?

(e) Is adequate labor of the right type available?

(f) Are utility costs comparable to those available at other potential sites?

(g) Are adequate shipping facilities available at minimum costs?

(h) Would alternative sites offer lower costs and increased profits?

(i) Is local government and community attitude conducive to this site?

2. Wholesaling

(a) Is the site suitably zoned?

(b) Is the site economically suitable to the market to be served?

(c) In both receiving and shipping goods would additional facilities (rail, truck, or air) reduce costs by improving efficiency?

(d) Does this site make the best possible use of plant layout to minimize labor costs?

(e) Do potential competitors have a cost advantage over you in receiving or delivery to their customers?

(f) If customers have to visit the site is there adequate parking and convenient access?

3. Retailing and service

(a) Is the site suitable with regard to your competition?

(b) Is it in a high traffic area and are neighboring stores doing a good business?

(c) Is it in an expanding market?

(d) If the competition is inefficient or unaggresive, what would an improvement in that inefficiency or aggressiveness do to this site?

(e) If parking is required, is it adequate and conveniently accessible?

(f) If location on a particular side of the street is important, is it on the best side?

(g) Are there any disadvantages to this site? In other words is there a more suitable site within this general area? For example, if the site is located between a used car lot and a take out restaurant, would it be a good spot for a plant shop?

(h) Is the market a stable or growing one? In other words consider population trends, payrolls, local attitudes.

(i) Is the site dependent on a seasonal business (for example, tourism)?

(j) In rented premises is it a high or low rent area?

(k) Is the rent competitive?

(l) If it is a low rent area and your competition is in a high rent area because of a more suitable site, how are you going to compensate for the low rent to attract business?

(m) Are the surrounding buildings in a state of good repair? If they aren't they may detract from your business.

(n) Is the area safe from vandals and is there good police and fire protection?

The population base and the number of competitors in the local trading area can be key considerations in finding a good site for a retail or service business.

Many studies have been conducted to show the general surrounding population that is needed to support different types of retail or service businesses. For example, each grocery store might need a population base of 800 to 1,000 people whereas a store specializing in photography supplies and equipment might need a population base of 40,000.

You should do your research and determine the population base for the particular type of business you are interested in and measure this against the number of competitors you may have to see if there is enough business for all of you.

You might also want to compare the pros and cons of a downtown location. In a downtown area there are generally more potential customers among those working in the area. However, what is critical is whether or not these potential customers can be part of your market. If not, then your market must be people from outside the area who are shopping downtown, in which case traffic and parking considerations are critical.

Also, in a downtown area you can expect major competition from large retail and department stores as well as higher rent and operating costs.

Downtown locations are often not good for evening and Saturday business since suburban dwellers usually prefer to visit their local shopping malls rather than drive downtown.

Locating in a shopping mall can create similar types of decision problems. Shopping malls have high rents, but they do generally attract plenty of traffic and potential customers and have good accessibility, plenty of parking, pooled advertising possibilities, and potential for future business growth.

In summary, selecting the right site involves skill, common sense, knowledge, good judgment, and an awareness of the requirements of a successful business, such as traffic patterns and circulation, business generators, building planning, real estate, and — probably as important as any — luck in site selection.

7

EVALUATION OF THE BUSINESS

For the seller: *Use this chapter to evaluate your own business so you can present it in a better light.*

Once you have a specific business in mind to buy, you must fully evaluate it to be sure that you really are making the right decision to move to the next step: arriving at a proposed purchase price and carrying out purchase negotiations.

Evaluating a business is an endeavor that requires time and effort, but that investment in time and effort will minimize the risk of buying a business that you will not be able to operate with financial success.

Not all of the questions raised in the following sections will necessarily be relevant in your case, but they may prompt other questions that are relevant.

a. REASONS FOR SELLING

The first step is to determine the reason the business is for sale. The reason could be one or more of the following:

- Owner's retirement or ill health
- Owner's desire to relocate
- Declining business because of poor location, obsolete products or services, changing economic or market circumstances, and similar reasons
- Additional financing required to improve or expand the business with the present owner unwilling or unable to raise this money
- Owner's frustration with inflation, regulations, union, suppliers, interest rates, creditors, consumer boycotts, etc.
- Owner moving on to a better business opportunity

- Business's inability to collect receivables
- Potential squeezing out of the market or takeover by a larger firm
- Newer, better products soon to be introduced by the business's competitors
- Run down premises and/or worn out equipment or excessive costs that no longer allow the business to be price competitive
- Loss of a license, a lease, a franchise, or a supply source
- Recent loss of key employees
- Location no longer viable because of changed traffic patterns, changed zoning bylaws, or similar situations
- Loss of major contracts
- Potential lawsuits
- New regulations (for example, pollution control) that are too expensive to install
- Local or national economic conditions creating a depressed market for the goods.

1. The real reason

There may be a reason or reasons for selling in addition to any in the above list. It is critical that you determine the real reason (and not just what the owner says is the reason) for selling. You don't want to have any later surprises, and the seller's reason for selling can probably be used to advantage in the eventual negotiation process.

For example, despite what the seller says, his or her objective may be to go into competition with you after the business is sold, particularly since the seller knows all about the business you will now be running. This would probably give the seller a decided competitive advantage.

To combat that you might want to protect yourself with a clause in the buy/sell contract that reads: "The seller agrees not to engage in any competitive business for a period of 5 years after the sale date within a range of 10 miles (16 km).

2. Further checks

In addition, check with suppliers, customers, the Chamber of Commerce, the Better Business Bureau, and zoning departments or other municipal officials to see if there are other possible reasons for the owner's desire to sell out.

Even if the owner thinks the business is no longer viable that does not mean it isn't a good investment opportunity for you. Your energy, knowledge, managerial skills, and other factors may allow you to run a very successful business. The present owner's problems may indeed be opportunities for you.

b. BACKGROUND OF BUSINESS

It will be useful to obtain as much background information about the business and its history as possible. You should have answers to the questions listed below.

1. General
- When was the business started?
- How many different owners has it had?
- How long has the present owner operated it?
- If there have been frequent changes of ownership what is the reason?
- Has the business earned a good reputation in the community and specifically with its suppliers, competitors, and neighbors?
- How effective has the present owner/operator been in the past few years? What can you do to be even more effective?
- Has the company lived up to all local bylaws? Are there any upcoming changes in bylaws that could affect your operation of the business?

2. Products/services
- Has it been good at marketing its products/services?
- Has it been good at gaining public acceptance on new products/services introduced?
- Is the company planning new products/services that you, as a prospective purchaser, will benefit from?
- Has the market for its products/services grown over the last few years, and is it expected to grow over the next few years?

- Is it in an industry that is historically stable? If so, do you anticipate this stability to continue?
- Is it in an industry that is historically cyclical or unstable? If so, at what stage is the present cycle? For example, if the industry is in a down turn, would you be able to survive if you purchased a business in it now?

3. Competitors
- Who are the competitors, and how has the business fared against them?
- Is the number of competitors in this industry decreasing or increasing? How do you anticipate competing with them in the future?
- How do the products/services of the company (in quality and price) compare with the competition's?
- If the company buys from a small number of sellers, or sells to only a small number of purchasers, how would the loss of a contract, or a supplier or purchaser going out of business, affect the company?

4. Employees
- Is the business badly organized and even overstaffed? Could there be cost savings in this area?
- Are employees fairly paid?
- If the company has a union, when does the contract expire? Are there any negotiations underway?
- Are employees generally satisfied? Has the employee turnover rate been high in the last few years indicating signs of low morale and general poor attitude of employees toward ownership/management?
- Have training/educational courses been made available to employees at no cost to them?
- What fringe benefits and incentive programs has the company been providing? Are these adequate for today and will you have to add to them?

c. EVALUATING ASSETS

It is quite likely that you will be taking over some of the present owner's assets, and for this reason you need to evaluate them. Some of the more common assets are discussed in the following sections.

1. Accounts receivable

If you are taking over accounts receivable outstanding at the purchase date, check back to see if there are any abnormal fluctuations in amounts of accounts receivable outstanding over the past few years.

Age the accounts. This means recording individual accounts in categories of age such as 30, 60, 90, or over 90 days old to determine how many might be uncollectible.

In particular look for large amounts of receivables from a few customers that have been outstanding for some time. Contact these customers directly to determine if they agree with the amounts owing. Verify invoices and signed shipping orders to ensure that customers have received the merchandise they are being billed for.

You need to carefully examine receivables that are outstanding for a considerable time since you, as purchaser, will be responsible for any bad debt losses if the debtors do not pay up.

One of the advantages of taking over collectible accounts receivable is that they will help you learn who the company's customers are and what their paying habits are.

2. Customer lists

Make sure you will have access to all the present owner's customer and mailing lists.

3. Supplier contracts

Check that you will be able to maintain the same supplier agreements or contracts as the present owner (assuming that you want them). For example, if the present owner has intentions of starting up a new competitive business, you wouldn't want him or her to take those agreements or contracts to the new business and find yourself unable to obtain the material or merchandise lines that the business has traditionally dealt with.

4. Licenses, leases, franchises

Will any licenses necessary for the business's operation be readily transferable to you? Normally, this would not be a problem, but there are situations (for example restaurant liquor licenses, and hair salon licenses) where you may not be able to simply assume the license.

Check into all the licensing requirements of your state or province and city governments to make sure you will be able to properly conduct the business subsequent to purchasing it.

With reference to a lease you will want to know if the present lease is transferable without renegotiation. If it is, find out the following.

(a)   How long does the present lease still have to run?

(b)   What renewal options are there, if any?

(c)   What rent escalation clauses are built into the lease?

Since the subject of leasing can be complex, it is dealt with as a separate topic in chapter 14.

Franchises are similar in some ways to leases. The same basic questions arise as with leases and the most important question is: will the franchisor transfer the franchise contract from the present owner to you? Again, since running a business under a franchise arrangement can be complex it is discussed in more depth in chapter 15.

5. Employees

Although you cannot put a dollar value on employees, good ones are an asset to any business. In particular, you should be interested in retaining good key employees in the business since they know the suppliers, the product lines, and the customers.

Can you find out how many of the present employees, particularly the key ones, will stay with the business after you take over? Would the business be able to survive during the critical takeover period if you lost these key employees?

Don't forget, it takes time and money to train new employees, and continuity of employment is valuable to any business and valued by customers.

6. Inventories

In a service business, the value of an inventory will be relatively small. However, in manufacturing and wholesaling, and to a lesser degree in retailing, it can be the largest single asset that you are taking over.

Indeed, a manufacturer may have three different types of inventory, each one a major asset: raw materials, work in process, and finished goods.

If inventories are a major asset that you are assuming, you need to be particularly careful about assessing the inventory value.

In some cases the seller's inventory may be worth more, because of inflation, than it shows on the books.

Even if you are purchasing a business that is unfamiliar to you, a physical assessment of the inventory is important. This physical examination will leave you, at the very least, with an impression of the worth of the inventory.

In addition, the following are some specific questions that you might want to have the answers to:

- Has the inventory value remained consistent over the past years? If it has not, what are the reasons?
- Has the ratio of average inventory to sales remained consistent over the past several years?
- How has the present owner arrived at an inventory valuation at the year end? Was it by a physical count and actual costing or by estimate only?
- Has the method of valuing inventory been consistent over the years, for example, lower of cost or market, last-in/first-out, first-in/first-out, or some other method? If different methods have been used for different categories, what method has been used for which categories?
- Are adequate inventory records kept that will verify the inventory valuations over the last few years?
- Is there any old, slow moving, or obsolete inventory included?

- Does the inventory contain any items on consignment that do not belong to the business you are buying since they have not been paid for?
- Does the inventory contain any items that have already been sold and recorded as sales, but not yet shipped?

If you are satisfied with the present owner's answers to these questions, you might be prepared to accept the present owner's valuation of current inventory on hand.

Alternatively, you might have to personally value the inventory or, if necessary, have an independent inventory appraisal carried out, possibly even using suppliers of the inventory if they are few in number and are willing to do this.

7. Prepaid expenses

Are you going to assume any prepaid expenses such as rent and insurance? If so, you should verify the contracts for these items and ensure that you can assume them.

In the specific case of insurance, you need to be sure the insurance policies can be transferred without loss of coverage or additional premiums and that insurance you do not wish to carry can be cancelled without penalty.

8. Fixed assets

Fixed assets include items such as land, building, machinery, and equipment. In particular you should be concerned about unnecessary deterioration of the building, machinery, and equipment. A physical inspection might show you their poor condition.

Another useful check is the income statement repair and maintenance expense figure. Frequently, owners who know they are going to sell the business, with its assets, will reduce the amount spent on repairs and maintenance. If the statement figures show that a declining amount has been spent in this area for the past months, or even years, this might indicate some run down assets.

You need to be assured that these assets will be able to produce efficiently and effectively after you take over the business. If not, your purchase price should be adjusted by the amount that will have to be spent in the immediate future on repairs and maintenance.

Also, consider these fixed assets from the point of view of expanding the business in the future. Will the land and building support a physical expansion? Can the machinery and equipment handle an increased capacity?

9. Intangible assets

Intangible assets include items such as patents and trademarks that will benefit the business in the future.

Find out if any exist on the books of the selling company. If so, do they really have any value? Patents have a limited life, and you should find out how much time is left before the patent expires. You should also ensure that any trademarks are registered. Trademarks, if registered, do not have a limited life.

d. FINANCIAL INFORMATION

Probably the most critical aspect in the evaluation of a company is its earning potential. As you will see in the next chapter, earning potential should form the basis of negotiating a buy/sell agreement acceptable to both parties.

Earnings are shown in the income (profit and loss) statements. Of course, you are only going to be able to obtain these statements from the present owner once you have gone through the rest of the evaluation and can convince the present owner that you are serious about making an offer for the business.

You should obtain these statements for at least the past three years, and even for as many as five. A key question to ask about the financial statements is who prepared them — the owner, an employed bookkeeper, or an outside professional accountant? Obviously, the latter would be preferable.

In fact, you should preferably have financial statements that are audited by a professional accountant since they will also be more acceptable to a bank or other financial institution from whom you may be seeking financing for your purchase of the business.

Wherever possible, these financial statements should be matched and verified with income tax returns.

Check or have your accountant check for inconsistency in financial statements (for example, sale of an adjacent piece of land owned by the company being shown as sales revenue rather than an extraordinary gain on the sale of an asset). Also, be aware that business owners, knowing they plan to sell the business, will increase the value of certain assets, compensating that with an increase in the owners' equity account. There is nothing wrong with that if the increase in the assets' value is justified. Just be sure that it is.

You must be sure the income statement figures are authentic. If you are not, you may be wise to discontinue your evaluation at this point and move on to greener pastures.

1. Ascertain trends

What you need to ascertain from the income statements are the trends of sales, expenses, and net incomes over the past three to five years. A declining trend of sales and profits would not be desirable. However, an increasing trend over the period may not truly be an increase after the figures are discounted for the effects of inflation. You must evaluate them with inflation in mind.

If you are familiar with the key income statement operating ratios (cost of sales percent, gross margin, inventory turnover, labor cost percent, net income to sales percent) for the type of business you are contemplating buying, you can see how the ratios of the company you propose buying compare. However, do this with caution since industry ratios are only an average and may not be indicative of success or otherwise of an individual company in that industry.

From the balance sheets of the company for the last few years you might also want to calculate some other important ratios (current ratio, acid test ratio, debt to equity ratio) and again compare them with industry averages.

2. Future earnings potential

Look at all these figures critically and see how you might be able to improve the business and its earnings potential. Keep any decisions you come to in this regard to yourself, since to show the seller how the profits could be improved is to increase the price tag to you as purchaser.

Alternatively, are there any new developments or market changes on the horizon that, although they might not deter you from buying the business, might make sales, expenses, and profit projections based on past earnings unrealistic? This would be an item for discussion in any buy/sell negotiations.

In the next chapter we will take a look at how the earnings figure of the business can be converted into a starting reference point for arriving at an eventual negotiated purchase price.

8

VALUATION METHODS

For the seller: *This chapter will explain how to establish a reasonable selling price for your business.*

In general terms, the value of a business is what the buyer is prepared to pay and what the seller is prepared to accept, as long as both are aware of all the facts and neither is under pressure to complete the transaction. However, this definition does not tell us how to determine a value that is fair to both parties.

a. VALUATION METHODS

There are a number of different methods available for helping to establish the value of a business. Some of these will be discussed below.

1. Book value method

The easiest way of calculating the value of a business is to determine the current book value of its assets from its balance sheet and deduct from that the liabilities. However, the book value (cost price less accumulated depreciation) of some assets may not reflect current market values if the business is more than a year or two old.

For example, existing equipment may have a value on the books, but the equipment may be obsolete and of little value if better equipment is now available. Also, book value of land at cost may not be realistic if inflation has caused land values to increase since the business began.

On the other hand, the book value of assets such as accounts receivable and inventory may be overestimated.

For these reasons the book value method is a risky one to use.

2. Cost or replacement method

The cost or replacement method approaches the problem by establishing the current cost that would be required to reproduce the building and equipment, subtracting from that a reasonable amount for depreciation caused by deterioration and functional or economic obsolescence, and then adding the current value of the land, inventory, and any other assets.

If the business is fairly new, this method might be reasonably accurate. However, the older the building, the more difficult it is to use the method accurately.

Also, the present value of a business is often quite independent of the present cost of putting up a similar building. In other words the economic viability of a business is usually more important in determining its value, and the cost method fails to recognize this.

3. Market method

The market method approach evaluates a business by comparing it with similar properties that have recently sold, in the same way that values of houses are established in buy and sell situations.

To make the assessment more accurate, the recent sales prices of comparable businesses have to be adjusted for such factors as age, type of building construction (frame versus concrete block), building and equipment condition, location (site), and layout.

Even if there were sufficient similar business sales occurring in the area, and even if accurate information were available about those transactions, the comparison is still extremely difficult.

Similar businesses differ widely in type, size, reputation, market served, managerial efficiency, and other intangible factors that make the market method very difficult to use with any degree of accuracy.

The major reason for this is that even if all the necessary data were readily available, it is difficult, if not impossible, to quantify most of it.

4. Liquidation value method

Another method of business evaluation is to determine its liquidation value. To use this method you need to calculate the net amount of cash that would be received if all assets were sold and liabilities paid off. In other words what would be realized in cash if the firm went out of business?

Unfortunately, this is not a realistic method since it does not reflect the goodwill value of the business if it stayed open. However, the liquidation value does show a price below which the seller would generally be unwilling to sell since that much cash could be realized by going out of business rather than selling it.

b. THE INCOME METHOD

A business for sale is both real estate (if land and buildings are involved) and earnings. It must be valued with this in mind.

The current balance sheet (showing the business's assets and liabilities) is not too useful in this exercise since the asset value for the major assets (such as land and building) may not show current value based on the future earnings potential of the business.

This is particularly true if the business is some years old, and it is for this reason that the valuation methods discussed so far fall short in establishing a fair market value in a buy/sell situation.

The income method overcomes this problem by basing the business's value on income or profit before depreciation, interest, and income taxes, and using an appropriate "capitalization" rate.

1. Income before depreciation, interest, and income tax (IBDIT)

Basically, the income method requires an estimation of the average future annual income of the business. The figure required is income before depreciation, interest, and tax (IBDIT).

Average future IBDIT is best estimated from the business seller's income statements (preferably audited), adjusting for future economic conditions and other factors.

One of those factors might be the salary of the present owner included in operating expenses. This figure should be taken out and replaced with a salary figure that you feel would be a reasonable one, given your circumstances, for managing the business.

Also taken into consideration in the estimate of IBDIT is the business's location (visiblity, accessibility, landscaping, and space for expansion where these are important), competitive position (product prices, supply and demand considerations, reputation, and goodwill), and a study of the physical property to determine exactly what facilities it does have and whether adequate maintenance has been carried out.

Although many of these items require a subjective judgment, they must be considered in establishing the business's value, and thus they must be included in the estimate of future IBDIT.

Also, the estimated IBDIT figure should include expenses that historical income statements have not recorded. For example, if the building to be purchased is badly run down as a result of improper maintenance, the estimated future IBDIT figure should be reduced by an increased maintenance expense.

Similarly, if it is obvious that the fixtures and equipment are in need of replacement over the next few years, then it might be appropriate to include a reserve for furniture and equipment replacement amount in calculating IBDIT.

Finally, if there are any nonrecurring items of income and expenditure (for example, the profit or loss from the sale of a major asset) in the historic figures these should be excluded in projecting IBDIT.

In projecting IBDIT, you must assume that there will be some good years and some bad years. The IBDIT figure will therefore be an average. Also you should not include in IBDIT any increased profit from any proposed further investment and expansion of the business since you should pay the seller only for what exists now.

2. Capitalization rate

Once IBDIT has been determined, it is divided by an appropriate capitalization rate.

The capitalization rate is generally weighted for a number of components. One of the components would be the current loan or mortgage interest rate that you expect to pay on any funds that need to be borrowed for the purchase.

A second component of the capitalization rate is the return on your equity in the business. The equity investment is the amount of money you actually put up yourself, that is, it is your own cash investment.

These two interest rates would be weighted by the ratio of the amount of investment from borrowed money (debt) and your equity.

For example, if 75% of the purchase price were borrowed at 16%, and on the balance of 25% of your own funds you wanted a 20% return, the weighted capitalization rate would be:

$$
\begin{array}{ll}
75\% \text{ debt} \quad \times 16\% = 12\% \\
25\% \text{ equity} \times 20\% = \underline{5} \\
\text{Total} \qquad\qquad\quad \underline{\underline{17\%}}
\end{array}
$$

To the mortgage component, and the return on equity component, could be added a third component: a risk factor. This risk factor can vary with each business buy/sell transaction, and it would be primarily a matter of opinion.

For example, in the above illustration the purchaser might want to add 3% for risk, making the total weighted capitalization rate 20% (17% + 3%) or 0.20.

3. Determining purchase value

Using the total weighted average capitalization rate an appropriate purchase value for the business can be determined. This is done by dividing the estimated annual IBDIT figure by the capitalization rate. Assuming the IBDIT was $175,000 and the capitalization rate 0.20, the business value would be:

$$
\frac{\$175,000}{0.20} = \$875,000
$$

The above calculation shows that a capitalization rate of 0.20 (or 20%) means that the value is five times IBDIT.

In fact, a capitalization rate of 20% is often used for the purchase of a small business that shows reasonable prospects for continued success and relatively low risk. If the prospects were quite risky, a capitalization rate as high as 100% could be used (i.e., value of one year's IBDIT). Note that the higher the capitalization rate used the lower the valuation arrived at, and vice versa.

c. NEGOTIATED PRICE

The purchase value figure arrived at is not necessarily the one that will result from seller/buyer negotiations. It is only the price that will fulfill the given assumptions. The negotiated price might, in fact, be higher or lower than the calculated figure. If higher, it will decrease the buyer's return; if lower, it will increase that return.

If the asking price for the business is much above or below the calculated value indicated in the IBDIT capitalization calculation, then further investigation may be necessary.

If the business is over-priced, it may have some special features that do not show up in the calculations.

If it is under-priced, it should signify a cautious approach to further negotiations. For example it may be operating under conditions that do not conform to local bylaws — particularly if these have been recently upgraded. In some cases of upgrading the current owner may be allowed to operate without conforming to the changes, but those changes may directly affect a new owner in bringing the business up to new standards of fire protection or other similar expensive matters.

When contemplating purchase of a property, it is a good idea to check with local regulatory authorities to verify potential cost problems that may arise with a change of ownership.

1. Purchase strategy

Once you have established in your own mind a purchase price that would be satisfactory to you, you might want to increase it by a factor of, let us say, 5% and put that as a ceiling price in negotiations.

Prior to actual negotiation you might want to reassess the seller's reasons for selling since they can dictate in part your negotiation strategy.

In fact, the nonfinancial demands of some sellers may be more difficult to negotiate than the financial terms. For example, what are the seller's views on —

(a) the reputation and prestige (goodwill) of the business,

(b) the value of the employees who are experienced in the business and will stay on, and

(c) the value of the operating and control systems already established?

Many sellers of small businesses find it difficult to sell without imposing certain conditions as if they were staying on in ownership! For example, they may want to ensure that their good employees will be guaranteed their jobs, that the quality of the products and services will not be altered, and that the same suppliers will still be used. In other words they don't want anything to change.

These conditions can, in fact, become part of your purchasing strategy. They can become negotiating points to lower the eventual purchase price.

Put yourself in the seller's position and try to determine what other issues are going through the seller's mind and then use them to advantage.

For example, would the seller really like to stay on in the business as an employee? If there appears to be compatibility between the two of you, and if you think the owner could now become an employee and not try to interfere in your management of the operation, you might want to have this occur — again with a possible reduction in purchase price for the business. Alternatively, it might be in your best interest to have the present owner stay on for awhile to help in the transition.

2. Contingent agreement

However, after all negotiations there might still be a wide difference between the seller's financial demands and what you think you can offer as a purchase price. At that point you might want to consider a contingent agreement or contract.

A contingent contract is an incentive agreement where your offering price is accepted on condition that if profits are higher than expected over the next, let us say, three years, the seller will receive additional contracted payments.

This can be rationalized on the basis that, even though the additional profits may be due primarily to your efforts, they are also improved by the continuing advice and expertise of the seller during the contracted period.

Alternatively, you might be willing to pay the seller's price if the seller is willing to carry some of the purchase price on a debt basis. This will reduce your equity and thus, through leverage (see chapter 12) you effectively increase your return on investment.

d. CASH FLOW

The topic of return on investment has been mentioned a number of times. However, you cannot calculate your real return on investment until after the final price has been agreed on and any necessary financing arrangements have been made. The subject of financing will be covered in the next four chapters.

To calculate your return on investment you must deduct from IBDIT an appropriate annual depreciation on any assets purchased, interest on any borrowed funds, and income tax. The resulting net profit figure, divided by your own equity investment, and multiplied by 100, will provide you with a return on investment percentage.

Even though the resulting return on investment figure is acceptable, you should then finally calculate your annual cash flow amount for the first several years. Profit is not the same as cash flow and it is critical that cash flow be calculated since it is the only figure that shows whether or not you will be able to pay back the principal amount on any borrowed funds.

If you are unfamiliar with how to calculate cash flow, your accountant can do this for you quite easily. Any cost involved will be well worth it since, if cash flow is not going to be positive in those early years, the price for the business will have to be renegotiated, your financing plan will have to be changed, or you may have to abandon your idea of buying that business.

9
WHAT'S INVOLVED IN FINANCING?

For the seller: *Help the purchaser put together financial information about your business to help in financing.*

While you are in the negotiation stage for the purchase of a particular business, and with some end price in mind, you might want to begin discussions with lending institutions for any required financing.

Knowing what's involved in securing financing can give you a distinct advantage. The most important fact to remember is that you are in competition with other people and other businesses for the same money.

It is often said that there is a shortage of funds for financing small businesses. However, what is more often the case is that many small business planners, owners, or operators are unfamiliar with the range of sources of funds and financial services available to them.

Another common complaint is that banks and other financial institutions insist on 100% plus guarantees of the success of the small business venture. The problem is that they are not provided with sufficient documented information to make a positive decision.

Therefore, being prepared, understanding the procedures involved, and having familiarity with the different types of financing available are the first steps in demonstrating good management of a financial proposal.

a. COMPETITION AMONG LENDERS
You should also understand that banks and other financial institutions are no different than you — they are in competition with each other in the same way you are with your competitors.

Banks make money by lending money at a profit. If they don't lend money, they don't make that profit. If you don't sell your goods or services, you won't make a profit. However, for a business to be profitable to the bank, the bank has to assess the risk in lending its money.

In borrowing money the words risk and interest are closely connected. Risk is the degree of danger the lender has in losing funds loaned to you. Interest is what you pay a lender for the use of borrowed funds. Normally, the higher the risk, the higher the interest rate that will have to be paid.

Decisions made by bankers are based on their judgment of the viability of your proposal. This judgment follows no secret formula (since banks do make errors in lending money that they cannot collect). However, bankers do require certain basic information to determine risk and make decisions.

This information is discussed in the following sections.

b. PREPARING THE PAPERWORK

The style and content of a loan application are of major importance when asking for a loan. To make the best impression on those approached for funding it is critical to have all the facts properly documented. Regardless of the type of loan, the information required by the lender will be basically the same.

The lender will want to know who you are, what your plans are, and what these plans will do for the business. The preparation of this information, in answer to the lender's questions, and the analysis that backs it up, is quite simple.

1. Resume of the owner(s)

In a planned purchase of an existing business, the lender will want to know something about you and any other owners, such as your education and experience (or lack of it) and how this will be valuable to the business.

The lender will want to be assured of your managerial skills. A past track record demonstrating ability in matters such as production, marketing, financing, and similar areas and how these can be related to the business you propose buying are some determining factors in assessing your management ability.

The lender can then compare, from his or her own experience in loaning money to other businesses, the relative strengths of your management.

2. Personal finance information

If you do not have a previous business track record, the lender will probably need personal financial information about you and the other owner(s). This information will show the lender what other financial support you can fall back on if the business is not immediately successful and requires further owner investment.

3. References

You will probably need to provide references, both personal and business. If you have dealt with other banks previously, references from them can be helpful, including details of any previous or present loans outstanding with those banks. The names of your accountant and lawyer are also useful for references.

4. Products and/or services

Information about the type of business that you are planning to buy will be required. This information could include the names of your suppliers and also the names of potential customers unless these would be unknown and large in number such as in a retail business.

The bank will want some details about the products and services of the company you propose buying. This includes information concerning sales trends of the products, their prices, their quality in comparison with competitors, and any proposed change in the product mix and the effect of that on profits.

With reference to future prospects the bank might want to consider the impact of environmental and/or technological change on the business you propose buying. Such factors as the availability of labor (if it is a labor intensive business), consistency of supply of required raw materials, and the adequacy of the present building and equipment to meet your projected future sales demands would be of concern to the lender.

An assessment of your market and potential market share could be included at this point. Finally, don't be reticent about including the names of your nearest competitors.

5. Financial statements

Financial statement projections will be required with detailed calculations showing, in particular, how total annual revenue is calculated and what the operating costs are projected to be. If you can provide copies of the seller's past financial statements, these will help support your projections and demonstrate your ability to repay any loan.

If a feasibility study has been prepared, it will serve to provide the lender with full financial projections for as many as five years ahead.

This financial presentation can be expanded by written explanations detailing each item, such as the size, location and legal description of the land to be purchased, a description of the building, and so forth. Firm items of cost should be specified, as should those that are only estimates.

The amount of your investment or equity in the business is important. Banks and other lending institutions do not finance 100% of the purchase of a business. You have to put some of your own money in — as much as 30% of the total cash required. If you are not prepared to risk your own money, why should the bank risk its funds?

6. Security offered

The prospective lender will want details of the security offered for any loan. This includes a description of the assets (land, building) to be bought, price you expect to pay, amounts of any mortgages you are going to assume that the seller has on these assets and the amount (if any) that has been paid toward these mortgages.

In particular, if a recent appraisal has been made on the land and building, it will be useful since it will indicate what the property is worth.

If the land and building are not to be owned, a lease agreement that you can assume might form the security offered. In such a case provide the lender with a copy of the lease agreement and a statement from the lessor showing that all rent payments already made (if any) have been made promptly.

7. Insurance policies

The lender will want to know if the business is adequately insured against losses and liabilities and, in each case, who the beneficiaries are. Therefore, copies of any insurance policies should be made available to the lender.

8. Other considerations

The importance of careful preparation of all the paperwork outlined above cannot be overstressed. The manner in which this information is professionally prepared (i.e., typed and in a clean cover) and presented to a potential lender will go a long way toward ensuring that the required funds will be obtained. (See the sample loan application in the Appendix.)

In calculations of sales and expenses, accuracy is critical. If careless errors are made in overestimating revenue or underestimating expenses (thus producing a "padded" profit amount), your credibility will be damaged. The chances of obtaining borrowed funds will be considerably decreased. For this reason professional help from a financial consultant or an accountant may be necessary.

Even though a suggested list of paperwork items has been outlined above it might be a good idea to contact potential lenders, in each specific case, to determine what they would like to be presented with.

This will ensure that time is not needlessly spent putting together a report that is far more than a lender is interested in or, alternatively, a report that fails to include some specific item that the lender does want.

When seeking financing it is a good idea to make appointments in a businesslike way with each potential lender. That is more likely to portray the image of a professional business operator than if you simply walk in the door and ask for money.

c. LENDING DECISIONS

When you apply for funds, there are two possibilities: the funding will be approved or denied.

1. Funding approved

If a request for financing is approved, find out everything you need to know about the conditions, terms, payment methods, interest rates, security requirements, and any front-end charges or fees to be paid. No commitment to accept the financing should be made until all this information is provided and understood and its impact on the proposed business purchase analyzed.

If financing is approved but with a requirement to meet certain other conditions, determine if these conditions are severe enough to restrict the operating standards desired. Will the conditions commit you to more than was intended, or are they normal financing requirements that were simply overlooked?

Once a final commitment is arranged, it is a good idea to provide the lender with future copies of financial statements. Frequently this will be one of the requirements for obtaining funding. Even if it is not, it will provide the lender with progress reports about the business and will be helpful to the lender in processing future applications for further financing.

2. Funding denied

If a request for financing is not approved, find out why. Use the lender's experience to your advantage. He or she will have reasons for not providing the financing. Lenders handle many requests for financing and have experience in the financial aspects of many businesses even if they do not have direct management experience.

For example, the lender might be able to see that your business will run into a shortage of working capital with the financial plan proposed. A shortage of working capital is one of the common reasons for failure of many small businesses. If a business is in trouble because of this, it is often difficult to obtain additional working capital assistance.

72

It is far preferable to ask for additional funds to strengthen working capital at the outset, and a potential lender may well be able to point this out as a possible problem with a proposed financing plan.

If there is something else wrong with the financing proposal, see if it can be corrected and then reapply. If not, use this knowledge when approaching other potential lenders or on future occasions when seeking funds.

10

LONG-TERM FINANCING

For the seller: *Guide potential buyers to financing sources.*

The major requirement in financing the purchase of a business is for long-term funds for assets such as the land and building and, to a lesser degree, long-life fixtures and equipment. This chapter discusses such long-term financing.

However, if you are buying a business in leased premises, the requirement for long-term financing is considerably reduced.

Therefore, if the type of business you are contemplating investing in does not require major long-term financing, you may wish to skim over some of the sections in this chapter.

a. DEBT VERSUS EQUITY

Although a variety of methods of raising long-term capital have been used by businesses, mortgage debt and owner equity are the two most common methods.

With debt, the lender does not have any equity or ownership in the business and thus normally has no active say in the day-to-day operations of the business. Banks are one type of debt lender. Their return on the investment (loan) made is the interest the business pays on the use of that money. The equity owners' return on their investment is usually in the form of dividends.

However, before you can raise any debt financing, you will normally have to show potential lenders that you are willing to invest (and risk) money in the business yourself. If you are not willing to invest in the business yourself by way of equity, then why should an outside lender invest by way of debt?

b. EQUITY FINANCING

The people who do have an active say in the day-to-day operations of the business are the equity investor(s) or the owner(s) of the company.

This equity investment could range from 10 to 50% of the total investment. The closer to 50% it is, the easier it will be to borrow and the higher your profits might be (since you will have less interest expense on borrowed money that will eat into those profits).

However, the higher the equity, the lower might be your actual return on investment since you are reducing the opportunity to trade on the lender's investment. This is known as using leverage, and will be discussed in chapter 12.

1. Personal funds

The most common source of equity capital is personal funds from savings. Over the past few years many entrepreneurs have been able to provide this initial equity because of inflation.

Inflation has caused their home values to increase to the point that the home could be remortgaged and provide a form of instant cash.

2. Friends or relatives

This equity could be further increased from the savings of friends willing to invest, or even from relatives (love money). However, many otherwise successful small business people have created problems by bringing in friends or relatives as investors.

Mixing social or family relationships with business is always risky, particularly if the business is not doing as well as everyone initially imagined, or if the terms and conditions of such loans are not clearly spelled out to prevent these lenders insisting on becoming involved in day-to-day operational matters.

To avoid these problems, make sure any friend or family loans are covered by written agreements, preferably drawn up by a lawyer. In this way agreements will at least be viewed by the lenders on a businesslike basis.

Agreement should be reached on such matters as rate of interest to be paid, when the loans will be retired (paid back), any option you have to pay them back early, and the procedures that all parties will follow if loans become delinquent.

Of course, if you have little or no initial equity and no friends or relatives to borrow from, you might have to opt for a business that requires little investment. Some service and labor intensive businesses may provide this opportunity. The labor provided will be your own (commonly called sweat money).

3. Loans versus shares

The equity investment could be in the form of stockholder loans, or common stock or shares in the company, or a combination of loans and shares. How the owners' or equity investors' investment in the company is structured will vary in each different situation.

However, generally speaking, the advantage of the money being invested as shareholder loans is that it can easily be paid back to lenders without tax, other than personal tax on interest you receive from the company before the loan is finally paid off.

If the money is in the form of shares, it is much more difficult to withdraw since shares must be sold to someone else and may be subject to capital gains tax.

On the other hand, shareholder loans, because of the ease with which they can be repaid, are looked upon with skepticism by banks and other debt investors since it would be feasible for you to borrow money from a debt lender and use the cash to pay yourself back your own loan investment.

The long-term debt investors may therefore place restrictions or conditions on when and how the company can pay off shareholder loans, redeem shares, or possibly even pay dividends on shares. These restrictions or conditions are imposed to protect the long-term debt investors.

In particular the advice of a tax accountant is suggested since your personal tax situation (and that of any other equity investors) and the degree of financial success of the business can have a bearing on whether the shareholders' investment should be in the form of loans or purchase of shares.

c. DEBT FINANCING

Where long-term debt is required, it will probably be in the form of a mortgage.

A mortgage is a grant by the borrower to a creditor or lender giving preference or priority in a particular asset.

If the borrower is in default (for example, for nonpayment of interest or principal owing), the creditor holding the mortgage is entitled to force the sale of the specific asset pledged as security.

Proceeds of the sale would go to the holder of the first mortgage before any other creditors would receive anything.

If another creditor had a mortgage on the same asset, he or she would be classified as a second mortgage holder and would rank below the first mortgage holder but above a third mortgage holder (if one existed) or other creditors of the borrower in default.

The legal procedure by which the first mortgage holder can force the sale is called foreclosure.

In the business world, first mortgage lenders are generally organizations that have collected savings from many individual investors or lenders. The organization, acting as an intermediary, combines these savings and lends them in lump sums.

Such organizations include insurance companies, pension companies, real estate investment trusts, commercial and mortgage banks, and even trust companies and credit unions.

1. Feasibility studies and other requirements

Before lending money, these organizations would consider the borrower's track record. A business operator with a proven record of five years or more of successful experience in business would be more likely to obtain funds at a reasonable rate than would a novice.

Lenders are also concerned about the amount of equity invested by the owner. This equity usually takes the form of a direct cash investment in shares if the company is incorporated. Without such equity investment, the mortgage lender is taking a very high risk.

As mentioned, such equity generally needs to be a minimum of 25 to 30% of the total required financing. In other words, if the total cost to purchase a business is $100,000 you need $25,000 to $30,000 of personal cash investment.

A prospective lender would also be concerned that proper accounting procedures, particularly for cost control, be instituted. Lenders frequently require audited financial statements at least yearly but sometimes more frequently. This allows them to read possible danger signs before it is too late.

Some lenders carry out on-site inspections of properties in which they have investments to ensure that the property is not run down and that it is being maintained adequately. This ensures that their investment is better protected. In some cases the mortgage investor may stipulate a percentage of annual revenue that must be spent on property maintenance.

2. Loan terms

Generally, first mortgages can be obtained for up to 70 or 75% of the appraised value of the land and building offered as security for the loan. If the land is leased, then the mortgage would usually be obtainable only on the appraised value of the building.

Loan terms are usually for a maximum of 20 to 25 years. However, the term could be as short as 10 years.

Repayment of loans is generally made in equal monthly payments of principal and interest. These payments are calculated so that, at the stated interest rate, the regular payments will completely amortize (pay off) the mortgage by the end of its life.

Sometimes the payments are calculated so that, during the early years, interest only is paid (with no reduction in principal.

3. Early prepayment

Most first mortgage loans do not permit any early prepayment for at least the first several years. Thus you are locked in for that period and cannot benefit if interest rates decline.

Where prepayment is permitted, the mortgagor may impose a penalty. The penalty is usually a percentage of the balance still owing, and the percentage may decline as time goes by. You might be prepared to pay such a penalty.

For example, if the initial mortgage carried an 18% interest rate, and current rates had declined to 14%, you might be able to negotiate a new loan with a new lender and use part of the proceeds to pay off the remaining balance of the initial mortgage plus penalty. The penalty imposition may be more than offset by the interest reduction over the term of the new mortgage.

Since circumstances in each case will differ, each decision about long-term mortgage refinancing must be made on its own merits.

4. Call provision

Just as you may be permitted early repayment opportunities to benefit from changed general market interest rates, the lender also is usually protected. Most mortgage agreements have a call provision in them.

This call provision allows the lender, after a stated number of years, to ask for complete repayment of the mortgage. The lender and borrower then renegotiate a new mortgage at a new interest rate for a further stipulated period of time. A lender would probably call a loan if interest rates had increased since the original mortgage agreement was signed.

There is also an increasing use of variable interest rate mortgages where the interest rate, depending on market conditions, can be changed up or down by the lender as frequently as monthly.

5. Other compensation

Some lenders also require additional compensation, such as a fee, discount, or bonus. For example, a $10,000 bonus on a $250,000 mortgage would mean you receive only $240,000 but must pay back principal and interest on the $250,000. Such front-end "loads" obviously raise the effective interest rate.

Other lenders may ask for an equity participation. Such equity participation increases the lender's return on investment and, at the same time, dilutes your return on investment. Equity might take the form of a percentage of annual revenue or an investment in common shares.

6. Joint venture

In some cases, the lender might enter into a joint venture agreement with you. Such an agreement might provide you with some equity funds (while giving up part of equity control) as well as mortgage funds.

In other cases, the mortgage investor might supply 100% of the total project cost for which he or she receives a substantial equity position. This might significantly reduce your capital outlay and at the same time reduce your risk, control, and potential future income.

7. Equipment and fixtures

Most long-term mortgage lenders will not normally finance any portion of the equipment and fixtures. The prime reason is that mortgage lenders are in the long-term loan business, and furniture and equipment have a relatively short-term life.

However, despite this, they will sometimes attempt to obtain a first mortgage on these chattels (in addition to the long-term mortgage on the assets they have financed).

In this way, if the first mortgage lender has to foreclose, he or she is sure that the equipment and fixtures will not be removed and that the business can continue to operate.

8. Second mortgages

Second mortgages are also used for financing land and building. A second mortgage lender would take a second lien on the property mortgaged. The loan amount is generally limited to 5 to 15% of the appraised value of the property, and loan terms usually range from 5 to 15 years.

Second mortgage interest rates are generally three to four points above first mortgage rates because of the additional risk involved. Repayments are made over the life of the loan in equal monthly installments of principal and interest.

An excessive second mortgage can be risky to both you and the lender because of potential cash flow problems if the business is not successful.

9. Personal guarantee

Finally, even if your business is incorporated, the mortgage lender may require your personal guarantee of the loan in the event your company does not meet its debt obligations. This means that if your company defaults on its repayments, the lender can claim against your personal assets, such as your savings, your home, and your car.

If that is the case, make sure that when the loan is paid off you obtain a release from the guarantee. If a personal guarantee is required by the lender in addition to other security, try to negotiate a guarantee only for the amount of the shortfall and not for the full amount of the loan.

Also, if you have made a direct loan to the company and were obliged by the debt lender to sign a postponement of claim for your own loan, make sure that the postponement of claim is also cancelled.

Similarly, if during the period of the debt, restrictions were placed on payment of dividends to you, or if life insurance policies were assigned to the lender, have these restrictions removed or the policies changed.

11

SHORT- AND INTERMEDIATE-
TERM FINANCING

For the seller: *Guide potential buyers to financing sources.*

In the preceding chapter, the subject of long-term financing was covered. That type of financing is primarily used for purchasing long-term assets, such as the land and building, with the asset becoming the security or collateral for the debt.

In this chapter, short- and intermediate-term financing is discussed. This type of financing is necessary to cover the purchases of assets having a much shorter life (equipment, fixtures, and furniture) and even to help pay for some other assets, such as inventory.

a. SHORT-TERM FINANCING

Some of the various methods of short-term financing are as follows.

1. Trade credit

Surprisingly, the most common means of short-term financing is trade credit or financial assistance from other companies with whom you do business. The reason for this is that most suppliers do not demand cash on delivery other than in those cases where a business has a reputation for delinquency in payment of accounts.

Usually a bill or invoice for purchases is sent at the month-end. In the case of, let us say, a 30-day payment period for items purchased at the beginning of a month this would mean that you use the service or supplies received without cost for anywhere up to 60 days.

To a business, this type of trade credit is an important source of cash. Even if you have the cash to pay the bill at the time it is received, it may not be wise to do so.

As long as there is no penalty imposed, you are free to let your cash sit in the bank and collect interest until the invoice has to be paid. This is another source of profit for you.

This type of trade credit is sometimes called "open credit" since it is generally arranged on an understanding between buyer and seller without any formal agreement in writing.

This credit is useful in financing the inventory of a business that you are buying. For example, if you purchased $25,000 of inventory, you might put up $10,000 cash and owe the suppliers the balance to be paid 30 days later. During that 30 days most if not all of that inventory will be sold at a profit and you will have the cash to pay off the $15,000 owed. This cycle can be repeated ad infinitum.

There are three typical methods of arranging payment with a supplier: cash on delivery (COD), no cash discount, and cash discount.

The first, COD, means in effect that the purchaser does not receive any trade credit. Cash must be paid at the time of delivery.

The second, more common arrangement is for the supplier to extend credit for a specific number of days after delivery of the goods, or after the month-end following delivery of the goods, with no cash discount permitted. In other words, the full amount of the invoice or invoices must be paid.

The third arrangement is for the supplier to offer both a credit period and a cash discount. One common type is referred to as 2/10, net 30. This means that you are offered a 2% discount off the invoice price if the bill is paid within 10 days. If the bill is not paid within the 10-day period, it must be paid within a further 20 days but without discount. This type of arrangement is made to encourage you to pay bills promptly.

With a 2/10, net 30 arrangement, you must seriously consider the cost of not taking the discount. For example, if you make a $1,000 purchase and pay within 10 days, the amount to be paid is $980. If the discount is not taken, you have the use of this $980 for a further 20 days. However, the cost of this is shown on next page:

$$\frac{\$20}{\$980} \times \frac{365}{20} = 37.2\%$$

This is an expensive form of financing. Even if you are short of cash, it might be wise to borrow $980 from the bank to pay within the discount period, since the bank interest expense would probably be considerably less than 37%.

2. Goods on consignment

Another type of trade credit is to obtain goods on consignment. This is common in certain types of business.

When you receive goods on consignment, the supplier retains ownership of them. You only pay when the goods are sold.

This type of arrangement is sometimes referred to as a floor plan.

3. Stretching payables

In the discussion so far it is assumed that you pay bills before the end of the supplier's payment period. If you delay paying beyond that date, you are using this "free" money at a further cost to the supplier.

For this reason, suppliers do not encourage the practice. Banks and other lending institutions also look unfavorably on businesses that make a habit of not paying bills promptly.

If you have this reputation, you might well find that suppliers will deliver only on a COD basis. You might also find it difficult to borrow funds when needed for short-term purposes.

However, if the nature of your business is seasonal, you might find it difficult to pay all bills in the off season when they are due. In such cases, it might be wise to arrange for a longer payment period with suppliers whose financial resources allow them to extend longer credit.

Alternatively, arrangements could be made with a lending institution to borrow funds for the interim period so that bills can be paid within the normal payment period.

You should also recognize that trade credit is not absolutely free. The supplier who extends credit also has financing costs, which must be paid out of revenue from the products sold. In other words, the cost is included in the selling prices. Where competition exists among suppliers, however, this hidden cost should be minimal.

4. Short-term or operating loans

Short-term or operating loans are for financing inventory, accounts receivable, special purchases, prepaid promotions and other items requiring working capital during peak periods. Normally up to 10% of annual sales can be borrowed to finance such requirements.

The main sources of short-term loans are commercial banks or similar financial institutions. Using a short-term loan is a good way to establish credit with a bank.

This type of loan could be secured or unsecured. The security might be any or all of the following:

- A fixed or floating charge debenture on accounts receivable, inventory, equipment, or fixtures. The lender can register this debenture in a similar way to a mortgage on land and building.
- A general assignment of your accounts receivable. You collect the receivables in the normal way unless you are in default of the loan. In that case, the lender assumes collection of the receivables. When receivables are assigned, you normally have to submit a list of the outstanding ones to the lender each month.
- An assignment of fire insurance and, in some cases, key employee life insurance policies.
- A personal guarantee by you and/or your spouse (when personal assets are registered in the spouse's name).

Short-term loans are usually negotiated for specific periods of time (for example, 30, 60, or 90 days, and less frequently for periods up to a year or more). They may be repayable in a lump sum at the end of the period or in periodic installments, such as monthly.

If you have adequate collateral, short-term loans of up to a year can sometimes be negotiated.

Each separate borrowing is usually covered by a promissory note (a form of contract spelling out the interest rate and terms of the loan), and the interest rate is frequently subject to change, particularly in erratic money markets.

Banks and other financial institutions vary interest rates according to money market conditions. The rates can change frequently. They also vary depending on the customer. The prime rate is generally the lowest rate available. Rates increase above that depending on the specific business, its credit rating, its size, and other factors.

It would probably not be unreasonable (because of the risk involved to the lender) to suggest that most small businesses in need of bank credit probably pay rates that tend to be among the highest.

The interest rate is usually a stated annual interest rate. The stated rate may differ from the effective (or true) rate if the loan is discounted. Discounting means that the interest on the loan is deducted in advance.

If a $1,000 bank loan is taken out at the beginning of the year to be repaid at the end of the year at a discount (interest) rate of 15%, you would receive $850 ($1,000, less 15% of $1,000, or $150) and repay $1,000 at the end of the year. Since you have only $850, the effective interest rate is:

$$\frac{\$150}{\$850} \times 100 = 17.6\%$$

The effective interest rate also differs from the stated rate if a loan is repayable in equal installments over the term of the loan rather than in a lump sum at the end of the loan period as in the case above.

Consider a $1,200 loan at a 12% rate, repayable in equal monthly installments of principal over a year ($100 per month) plus interest. If the interest is calculated on the initial loan, it will be 12% of $1,200, or $144 ($12 per month).

The effective rate of interest will be higher than the stated 12%, however, since you do not have the use of the full $1,200 for the year.

There are tables (available at most bookstores) from which you can figure out an exact rate of interest under various circumstances, but you can quickly calculate an approximate effective rate of interest.

With equal monthly repayments, on average the borrower has only half the $1,200 for use over the year, or $600 ($1,200 divided by 2). The effective interest rate is then:

$$\frac{\$144}{\$600} \times 100 = 24\%$$

This is double the stated rate.

In all cases where money is being borrowed, and particularly where you are shopping around for the best rate, it is important to know what the effective interest rate is.

5. Line of credit

A line of credit is an agreement between you and a bank, or similar financial institution, specifying the maximum amount of credit (overdraft) the bank will allow you at any one time.

Credit lines are usually established for one-year periods, subject to annual renegotiation and renewal, with the bank taking your accounts receivable and inventory as security.

Generally, accounts receivable, as long as they are not overdue, may be financed up to 75% and inventory up to 50%.

The amount of credit is based on the bank's assessment of the creditworthiness of the company and its credit requirements. This type of loan is sometimes called a demand loan since the bank can demand that it be repaid immediately without notice and may be secured by you assigning your receivables to the lender.

b. INTERMEDIATE-TERM FINANCING

Somewhere between short- and long-term financing is a need at times for intermediate-term financing for items not generally purchased on a regular basis.

A common way to obtain this intermediate-term financing is through term loans. Installment financing is another possibility.

1. Term loans

Term loans are usually obtained from banks or similar financial institutions, but, unlike short-term loans, are usually arranged to cover the purchase of basic inventory, leasehold improvements, and assets like furniture, fixtures, and equipment.

Generally, 60 to 75% of the cost of these items can be obtained through term loans.

Term loans are usually repaid in regular installments of principal and interest over the life of the loan, which is usually less than the life of the assets for which financing is required. Term loans could vary in length from one to five years.

The interest rate on term loans is usually a percentage point or more higher than that for a short-term loan made to the same borrower.

The periodic payments on term loans can be geared to the business's cash flow ability to repay. In some cases, only the interest portion of such loans is payable in the first year or two. Payments could be monthly, quarterly, semiannually, or annually. Payments are calculated so that the debt is repaid (amortized) by a specific date.

If the periodic payments do not completely amortize the debt by the maturity date, the final payment will be larger than the previous periodic payments. This larger, final payment is known as a balloon payment.

Term loans sometimes allow early repayment without penalty.

Sometimes personal term loans are available to help finance your initial equity investment in the business. However, this can be risky since the total interest cost on all loans (since none of the money is your own) can be crippling to the company's working capital.

2. Installment financing

Installment financing can be used to finance the purchase of equipment of various kinds, including automotive equipment, and fixtures (such as counters, shelves, and display cases) where term loans are unavailable.

Although some furniture and equipment sales companies may finance this way directly, others will sell to a financing company that, in turn, will do the installment financing.

Many supply companies will act as an intermediary between you and the finance company to coordinate the arrangement. In other cases, you may have to shop around to arrange your own installment financing.

Since the assets being financed generally have a life of five to ten years, and since the financing agency runs a relatively high risk because of the very low value of second-hand furniture and equipment (and thus its low value as collateral), the length of life of such financing is usually from three to seven years.

There is usually a sizable down payment on such arrangements (from 20 to 30%), and the interest rate is generally much higher than with term loans. It could run as much as five or six points over prime.

Installment loans of this type are generally secured by a chattel mortgage (a lien on the assets financed), which can be registered and which permits the lending company to sell the liened assets if the installment payments are in default.

Alternatively, the lender's security could be by way of a conditional sales contract, whereby the lender retains title to the assets until you have satisfied all the terms of the contract.

12

VENTURE CAPITAL
AND OTHER FUNDING SOURCES

For the seller: *Guide potential buyers to financing sources.*

Apart from the traditional lending institutions that have been discussed so far, you might want to consider the following possible sources of funding.

a. VENTURE CAPITAL

A number of investment organizations, known as venture capital companies, specialize in funding small businesses. The term small, in this case, does not mean really small. Generally, venture capitalists are only interested in making loans in the $100,000 to $500,000 range for any single venture.

Since these investment companies are more interested in financing ongoing companies rather than funding brand new ventures, they might well be interested in helping you with the purchase of a successful ongoing business, particularly if you have plans to expand it.

Venture capital is available from these companies in both debt and equity form, although it is more common for them to take an equity position (common or preferred shares) since that allows them to participate more easily in the extra profits from the growth of your company.

Normally, they would look for a 20% a year compound rate of growth in your profits and a good likelihood of capital gain on their share holdings in your company.

Extracting funds from venture capitalists is not easy. They receive many more applications from people than they can ever fund. If you are one of the lucky ones, you can expect them, as one of the conditions, to want a say in how your business is operated, although their general security is how well you manage the business.

b. SMALL BUSINESS ADMINISTRATION (U.S.)

In the U.S., if all else fails you might want to consider the Small Business Administration (SBA). The SBA was created in 1953 by the federal government to succeed several predecessor agencies responsible for assisting entrepreneurs. Since that date, the SBA has expanded to embrace many activities. Its functions include, among others, finance and investment.

The SBA is organized into 10 regions and each region is subdivided, providing district or branch offices in many diverse centers of population.

SBA guidelines defining who qualifies for small business assistance vary, depending on the general classification of the enterprise. At the present time, the eligibility of a business is measured by number of employees or by sales volume or revenue. For example, the upper limit is $14.5 million per year for retail/service businesses.

As the lender of final resort, the SBA tries not to compete with or replace the private banking system but to supplement it. Loans made by SBA generally mature in 10 years or less for fixtures and equipment, and they are repaid in equal monthly installments of principal and interest, although this time period may be extended to 20 years where the purchase of land or a building is concerned. Working capital loans can be made for periods up to seven years. Regardless of the term, the loan may be repaid at any time prior to maturity without penalty.

Security on an SBA loan may be in the form of one or more of the following:

(a) A mortgage on the land or building, including the borrower's own residence.

(b) A chattel mortgage on the business's furniture and equipment

(c) Personal guarantees of the business's owner or owners

(d) Assignment of warehouse receipts for marketable merchandise

(e) Assignment of accounts receivable

There are three types of loans available from the SBA: guaranteed loans, immediate-participation loans, and direct loans.

1. Guaranteed loans

Since the philosophy of the SBA is that the private banking industry is the basic mechanism for the distribution of debt financing to small business, loans are made to a business by a bank or similar lending institution, but at a reduced risk because the SBA guarantees to pay part of any loss the lending bank might suffer.

Under the guaranteed loan arrangement, up to 90% of a loan may be guaranteed, or $500,000 — whichever is less.

The interest rate charged by a bank for a guaranteed loan may not exceed the prime rate by more than 2¼% for loans of less than seven years maturity or the prime rate plus 2¾% for loans of more than seven years.

The actual interest rate is negotiable, but the majority of loans tend to be near the high end of the range. In rare cases, it may be possible to borrow at or even below the prime rate. This could occur in a chain franchise operation because of the financial strength of the franchisor.

2. Immediate-participation loans

In cases where a guaranteed loan cannot be arranged, an immediate-participation loan may be available. With this type of loan, the SBA and the bank each provide a portion of the loan. For example, the bank may lend the major share of the funds required and be permitted to charge interest up to 2¾% over prime.

This interest rate is negotiable and could even be a fluctuating rate as market conditions change. The balance of the loan is from the SBA, and its interest cost is based on the government's cost of funds but by statute cannot exceed a rate that is 1% less than the maximum rate banks are allowed to charge on guaranteed SBA loans.

3. Direct loans

Direct loans are generally arranged at interest rates slightly lower than those on SBA sponsored bank loans. Direct loans may not exceed $150,000 without special approval, and in no case can they exceed the maximum limit of $350,000 established by statute.

Since direct loans are derived from a limited pool of funds, the availability of those loans is quite restricted. In the majority of cases, application for a direct loan is only made after the prospective borrower has demonstrated that credit is not otherwise available.

Since the SBA's regulations do change from time to time, you should verify current conditions by contacting your nearest branch of the SBA (listed in your telephone directory under U.S. Government) or write to:

Small Business Administration
Washington, DC 20416

c. SMALL BUSINESSES LOANS ACT (Canada)

In Canada, if all other sources of funding fail, you might want to consider the Small Businesses Loans Act (SBLA). The SBLA is available to small business enterprises. For purposes of the act, a small business is one whose annual gross sales are not over $2 million.

Most businesses are eligible for funding under the SBLA unless they are engaged in finance or in a profession, and as long as the loan is not for working capital requirements or to repay an existing loan.

Loans are available for:

- The purchase of fixed or movable equipment, including cost of installation, and the renovation, improvement or modernization of equipment where this is appropriate
- The purchase or construction of new premises or the improvement or modernization of existing premises in which the business is carried on or about to be carried on
- The purchase of land for the operation of a business, including the purchase of a building thereon

In other words, loans cannot be used for working capital, although you may be able to refinance any existing debt that you assume from the seller.

At the present time, the maximum amount that you may borrow under the act at any one time is $100,000. Subject to this maximum, loans can be used to finance up to —

(a) 80% of the cost, including installation, of fixed or movable equipment,

(b) 90% of the cost of the purchase or construction of new premises or the purchase of land, or the renovation or improvement of existing premises.

The rate of interest on SBLA loans is 1% over the prime lending rates of the chartered banks and fluctuates with changes in the prime rate during the term of the loan.

The maximum term of the loan is 10 years. Installments on a loan must be paid at least annually, or more frequently if required by the lender.

All SBLA loans must be secured. Security can take the form of land or chattel mortgages or other security the lender deems necessary. You will also have to sign a note promising to repay the loan. Depending on the circumstances in each case other conditions may be required.

All chartered banks and Alberta Treasury Branches are authorized to make loans under the SBLA. In addition, loans may be made by credit unions, caisses populaires, or other cooperative societies, trust companies, loan companies, and insurance companies, which have applied and have been designated as lenders under the act.

Therefore, if all other sources fail, talk to your own banker or other lender about the SBLA, and obtain a credit application. If you want further information about SBLA, write to:

Small Businesses Loans Administration
Department of Regional Industrial Expansion
235 Queen Street
Ottawa, Ontario
K1A 0H5

d. FEDERAL BUSINESS DEVELOPMENT BANK
(Canada)

You should also be aware in Canada of the Federal Business Development Bank, or FBDB. This lender is sometimes referred to as the lender of last resort. It was established by the government especially to help those companies that could not obtain financing elsewhere.

If your funding application has been turned down by other financial institutions, you may apply to the FBDB.

To obtain FBDB financing, the amount of your investment in the business must generally be sufficient to ensure that you are committed to it and that the business may reasonably be expected to be successful.

FBDB financing is available as loans, loan guarantees, equity financing, leasing, or any combination of these methods, in whatever way best suits the particular needs of your business. If loans are involved, they are usually at interest rates in line with those of other banks. If equity is involved, the FBDB generally takes a minority interest and is prepared to have you buy back its equity on suitable terms when the business is able to do this.

Most of the FBDB bank's customers use funds to acquire land, buildings, or equipment, although it is possible to use those funds to provide a healthy working capital for the business.

Financing from the FBDB can range from a few thousand to $100,000. Not many loans are made in excess of that amount. The amount that can be borrowed for a specific purpose depends on your ability to satisfy the bank's general requirements.

Also, once you have arranged financing from the FBDB, there is nothing to prevent you from returning and requesting further funding at a later date.

The FBDB also offers management counselling, management training, and other business information services including CASE (Counselling Assistance for Small Enterprise).

The purpose of CASE is to assist owners and managers of small businesses to improve their methods of doing business. To be eligible, you can already be established or about to be established in business in Canada. One restriction is that you must not have more than 75 full-time employees. There is also a nominal daily charge for this service. If you wish to pursue this, contact your local branch of the FBDB, or write to:

Federal Business Development Bank
P.O. Box 335
Stock Exchange Tower
Montreal, Quebec
H4Z 1L4

e. FINANCIAL LEVERAGE

In an earlier chapter, the concept of financial leverage, or trading on the equity, was introduced. To illustrate this, consider the case of a building that two partners are considering leasing for business purposes. Their investment would be $250,000 (for equipment and working capital).

The two partners have the cash available, but they are considering not using all their own money. Instead, they wish to compare their relative return on equity based on using either all their own money (100% equity financing) or using 50% equity and borrowing the other 50% (debt financing) at a 10% interest rate.

Regardless of which financing method they use, sales will be the same, as will all operating costs. With either choice, they will have $50,000 profit before interest and taxes.

There is no interest expense using 100% equity financing. With debt financing, interest will have to be paid. However, interest expense is tax deductible.

Assuming a tax rate of 50% on taxable profit, Chart #1 shows the comparative operating results and the return on the partners' investment (ROI) for each of the two options.

In this situation, not only do the partners make a better ROI under a 50/50 debt/equity ratio (15% ROI versus 10%), but they still have $125,000 cash that they can invest in a second venture.

Therefore, you could ask, if a 50/50 debt to equity ratio is more profitable than 100% equity financing, would not an 80/20 debt to equity ratio be even more profitable? In other words, what would the ROI be if the partners used only $50,000 of their own money and borrowed the remaining $200,000 at 10%? Chart #2 shows the result of this more highly levered situation.

Under this third option, the ROI has now increased to 30%, and the partners still have $200,000 cash — enough for four more similar business ventures.

1. Advantages of leverage

The advantages of leverage are obvious: the higher the debt to equity ratio, the higher the ROI will be. However, this only holds true if profit (before interest) as a percent of debt is greater than the interest rate to be paid on the debt.

For example, if the debt interest rate is 10%, the profit before interest must be more than 10% of the money borrowed (the debt) for leverage to be profitable.

With high debt (high leverage), there is a risk. If profit declines, the more highly levered the business is, the sooner it will be in financial difficulty. In the 50/50 financing in Chart #1 (relatively low leverage), profit before interest and income tax could decline from $50,000 to $12,500 before net profit would be zero. In Chart #2 (relatively high leverage), profit before interest and income tax could decline from $50,000 to only $20,000.

Therefore, in your financing plan, consider the mix of various sources of financing keeping the effects of leverage in mind. Big businesses make effective use of leverage. A small business can do it equally well.

CHART #1
EFFECT OF LEVERAGE ON ROI

	100% equity	50% equity 50% debt
Total investment required	$250,000	$250,000
Debt financing at 10%		$125,000
Equity financing	$250,000	125,000
Profit before interest and tax	$ 50,000	$ 50,000
Interest expense 10% x $125,000		(12,500)
Profit before tax	$ 50,000	$ 37,500
Income tax 50%	(25,000)	(18,750)
Net profit	$ 25,000	$ 18,750
Return on partner's investment	$\dfrac{\$\,25{,}000}{\$250{,}000} \times 100 = 10\%$	$\dfrac{\$\,18{,}750}{\$125{,}000} \times 100 = 15\%$

CHART #2
EFFECT OF HIGH LEVERAGE ON ROI

Total investment required	$250,000
Debt financing at 10%	$200,000
Equity financing	50,000
Profit before interest and tax	$ 50,000
Interest 10% x $200,000	(20,000)
Profit before tax	$ 30,000
Income tax 50%	(15,000)
Net profit	$ 15,000
Return on partners' investment	$\dfrac{\$15{,}000}{\$50{,}000} \times 100 = 30\%$

13

THE BUY/SELL CONTRACT

For the seller: *Pay particular attention to the details of your contract.* After you have made arrangements for any necessary financing for the purchase of the business, you will be ready to sign a buy/sell contract.

It is assumed at this point that the buy/sell price is firm, that purchase terms have been agreed to, that specific assets and liabilities to be transferred are also agreed to, and that both parties understand the income tax implications of the sale. Income tax implications will be discussed later in this chapter.

It is also assumed that, where relevant, you have verified the following: titles, deeds, contracts, mortgages, leases, licenses, patents, copyrights, union contracts, warranties, any liabilities you may assume (trade accounts payable, notes payable, accrued taxes payable, income taxes payable, long-term liabilities, unrecorded liabilities, contingent liabilities, and unearned revenues), and all similar matters including the franchise agreement if it is a franchised operation you are buying (the subject of franchising will be covered in chapter 15).

As buyer you are in a somewhat uncertain position at this point since, although you think you know what you are getting, some things may be uncertain. For example:

- What if the seller's financial statements turn out to be less than accurate?
- What if some of the assets to be purchased are not fully owned by the seller or have undisclosed liens on them?
- What if the seller has undisclosed liabilities?
- Could there be significant changes in the business between the time the agreement is signed and the transfer actually occurs?

- Could the seller already own a competitive business in the same neighborhood?

The seller, although knowledgeable about what is being sold, could also have uncertainties since, for example, he or she may be carrying some of the financing for the sale and is unsure of your ability to maintain payments.

For these reasons, a detailed contract is necessary, prepared by a lawyer, so that the interests of both parties are protected and all legal requirements are met.

a. TYPICAL CONTRACT

A typical buy/sell contract for a retail store is illustrated at the end of this chapter. Some comments about this contract are as follows.

Section 1 — Sale of business

Included in the buy/sell contract should be the conditions that explain the transfer of the business assets to you. The contract should clearly and specifically spell out which assets are being transferred and at what price. This is important for recourse against the seller in the case of missing assets or defects in the title.

Section 2 — Buyer's assumption of lease

This section documents that the buyer will assume the lease on the property previously held by the seller.

Section 3 — Method of payment

This section explains how and when the cash for the business is to be paid.

Section 4 — Adjustments

The adjustments section is similar to the clause in a residential sale contract that adjusts for items like property taxes or water bills that have been paid in advance. However, in a business situation the number of adjustments can be considerable.

Section 5 — Seller's warranties

This section protects the buyer from unexpected things like false or fraudulent information, undisclosed or potential liabilities or liens, and title defects.

Section 6 — Seller's obligation pending closing

This section is concerned with the time period between contract signing and closing or actual transfer of the business. The subsections are straightforward except, perhaps, for subsection (c).

This subsection complies with the bulk sales law of this jurisdiction. This law is to ensure that the seller does not sell out, pocket the proceeds, and disappear, leaving creditors unpaid. The seller must supply the buyer with a list of creditors, and the buyer must give notice to the creditors of the pending sale of the business.

Also, subsection (e) gives the buyer an opportunity to become familiar with the business prior to taking over.

Section 7 — Risk of loss

This section is concerned with the possibilty of a fire or similar event between contract signing and closing and what the status of the buy/sell agreement will be then.

Section 8 — Covenant not to compete

This section is to protect the buyer from suffering a loss of the business's goodwill if the seller were to go into competition with the buyer. This provision must be reasonable to be legally enforceable. What is reasonable depends on the circumstances in each case.

Section 9 — Conditions precedent to closing

This section is inserted because of the time difference between contract signing and actual closing. In this period, the purchaser could discover facts that could be cause for cancellation of the agreement. Because of this, good faith generally has to prevail for closing to occur. The only way around this is to have signing and closing occur at the same time.

Section 10 — Closing
This section explains where and when closing will occur.

Section 11 — Indemnification by the seller
This section obliges the seller to refund the buyer the full cost or damages suffered by the buyer if the seller is in breach of contracted obligations after closing.

Section 12 — Seller's security deposit
This section requires part of the purchase price to be placed in escrow as security for the seller's performance.

Section 13 — Arbitration of disputes
This final section provides a vehicle for resolving, without litigation, any disputes between buyer and seller that may arise from the contract.

b. ALLOCATION OF PURCHASE PRICE TO ASSETS

It is very important to you that the contract break down the total purchase price paid for the various types of assets (land, building, machinery, equipment, and goodwill). The reason for this is depreciation.

The cost of certain assets can be depreciated for income tax purposes, while the cost of other assets cannot (for example, land). But even assets that can be depreciated have different maximum annual percentages of depreciation that can be applied.

Obviously, you would normally prefer to record on your books that the entire purchase price was for assets, such as machinery and equipment, with high depreciation allowances (since this reduces your taxable profits and increases cash flow) and everything else (assuming there were other assets, such as land and building) was thrown in for nothing. This way you could take maximum advantage of a high rate of depreciation.

By the same token the seller will wish to show on his or her records that your full purchase price was paid for land (a nondepreciable asset) that would not be subject to a recaptured depreciation tax.

For these reasons it is necessary for buyer and seller to come to some agreement concerning the breakdown of the assets.

If the breakdown of the assets is not made in the contract, you may later find it very difficult to arbitrarily assign a cost breakdown that is convincing to the tax department.

1. Reasonable breakdown required

The breakdown of purchase price should be reasonable to both parties. It would be unreasonable for the seller to insist that you take over all tangible assets at their book value (particularly if they had been depreciated down to zero) with any balance of the purchase price being solely for goodwill.

It would also be unreasonable for you to insist that most of the purchase price be put into machinery and equipment if the land that goes with the purchase has a good market value.

Reasonable values would therefore be ones that had some bearing on market prices. This would not be difficult to determine for land, and a professional appraisal will provide a price for the building.

Machinery and equipment may be more difficult to valuate, but it might be possible to contact the original suppliers for an estimate of their current trade-in value. If any automotive vehicles are involved, the dealer will probably be able to provide current trade-in values.

If inventory is being purchased, it might be necessary to take an actual inventory count and value it from purchase invoices.

After all assets have been valued, there might still be a difference between the total of those assets and the purchase price to be paid. This difference could be used to adjust the figures of certain types of assets up or down or, if the purchase price is greater than the total value of the assets, the difference could be shown in the contract as goodwill.

Since depreciation can be a tricky subject, and since the rules and regulations about it can change from time to time, you should make sure your tax accountant is in on any discussions concerning this aspect of the buy/sell transaction.

c. BUYING SHARES INSTEAD OF ASSETS

You will note that nowhere in this chapter has it been suggested that (assuming the seller has a limited company) you might want to consider taking over the company by buying all its outstanding shares for whatever price buyer and seller negotiate the business to be worth.

If the subject is ever raised by the seller, DON'T DO IT!! There are two good reasons for this:

(a) The seller's company may have all kinds of liabilities (debts, tax liens, lawsuits) that have not been disclosed to you and that you would be liable for if you took over the shares in the company.

(b) The seller's company may have written all its depreciable assets down to zero, and you would have no base for further depreciation as you would have if you negotiated values for these assets and showed this in the contract. Therefore, buy assets, not shares.

However, if you are in a tax position where it might pay you to be able to use the seller's previous years' tax losses against future profits that you make there could be a case for buying shares but ONLY after you and your tax accountant have discussed the situation and considered all the tax implications.

SAMPLE AGREEMENT

This agreement is made and entered into this 28th day of November, 198_, between Sally Seller, hereinafter referred to as the SELLER, and Billy Buyer, hereinafter referred to as the BUYER.

Whereas the Seller is the owner of a souvenir shop under the trade name of Sally's Souvenir Shop in Anytown, and the Seller desires to sell to the Buyer her rights, title, and interests including the goodwill therein, and the Buyer is willing to buy

---

the same on the terms and conditions hereinafter provided, it is agreed as follows:

1. SALE OF BUSINESS

The Seller shall sell and the Buyer shall buy, free from all liabilities and encumbrances except as hereinafter provided, the souvenir shop owned and operated by the Seller under the name of Sally's Souvenir Shop at the premises known as 65 Lonsdale St., Anytown, including the equipment and fixtures, inventory, supplies, the goodwill as a going concern, and the lease to such premises, all of which are more specifically identified in Schedule A attached hereto. The purchase price for all the assets referred to above shall be allocated as follows:

Equipment and fixtures	$43,000
Inventory	12,000
Supplies	2,000
Goodwill	8.000
Total	$65,000

2. BUYER'S ASSUMPTION OF LEASE

In the event this agreement to sell is in fact closed and the business is transferred by the Seller to the Buyer, the Buyer shall be bound by and does hereby assume the terms of the lease of the building premises dated January 1, 198_ and the Buyer shall indemnify the Seller against any liability or expense arising out of any breach of such contract occurring after the closing.

3. METHOD OF PAYMENT

The Buyer shall pay to the Seller the purchase price as stated above in the following manner:

(a) $10,000 by certified check upon execution of this agreement, the receipt of which is hereby acknowledged by the Seller, such proceeds to be held in escrow by Jack D. Jack, lawyer for the Seller, as provided in Section 12.

(b) $55,000 by certified check at the date of closing, subject to the adjustments provided for in Section 4.

4. ADJUSTMENTS

Adjustments shall be made at the time of closing for the following: inventory sold, supplies used, payroll and payroll taxes, rent, insurance premiums, and deposits with utility companies. The net amount of these adjustments shall be added or subtracted, as the case may be, from the balance due on the purchase price at the time of closing.

5. SELLER'S WARRANTIES

The Seller warrants and represents the following:

(a) That she is the owner of and has good and marketable title to all the assets specifically enumerated in Schedule A, free from all debts and encumbrances.

(b) The financial statements that are attached hereto as Schedule B have been prepared in conformity with generally accepted accounting principles and present a true and correct statement of the financial condition of said business as of October 31, 198_.

(c) There are no business liabilities or obligations of any nature, whether absolute, accrued, contingent or otherwise, except as and to the extent reflected in the balance sheet of October 31, 198_.

(d) The statements made and information given by the Seller to the Buyer concerning said business, and upon which the Buyer has relied in agreeing to purchase said business, are true and accurate and no material fact has been withheld from the Buyer.

(e) The Seller has no knowledge of any developments or threatened developments of a nature that would be materially adverse to said business.

(f) No litigation, government proceeding or investigation is pending, or to the knowledge of the Seller threatened or in prospect, against or relating to said business.

6. SELLER'S OBLIGATION PENDING CLOSING

The Seller covenants and agrees with the Buyer as follows:

(a) The Seller shall conduct the business up to the date of closing in a regular and normal manner and shall use her best efforts to keep available to the Buyer the services of her present employees and to preserve the goodwill of the Seller's customers, suppliers, and others associated with the business.

(b) The Seller shall keep and maintain an accurate record of all inventory items sold in the ordinary course of business from October 31, 198_ to the date of closing. This record shall be the basis for adjustment of the purchase price as provided in Section 4.

(c) The Seller shall comply to the satisfaction of the Buyer's lawyer with all the provisions of the Bulk Sales Act of the _____ of _____ .

(d) The Seller shall deliver to the Buyer's lawyer for examination and approval prior to closing such bills of sale and instruments of assignment as in the opinion of the Buyer's lawyer shall be necessary to vest in the Buyer good and marketable title to the business assets and goodwill of the Seller.

(e) The Seller shall give the Buyer or his representative full access to the business premises, records and properties during normal business hours, and shall furnish the Buyer with such information concerning the operation of the business as the Buyer may reasonably request.

7. RISK OF LOSS

The Seller assumes all risk of destruction, loss or damage due to fire or other casualty up to the date of closing. If any destruction, loss or damage occurs and is such that the business of the Seller is interrupted, curtailed or otherwise materially affected, the Buyer shall have the right to terminate this agreement. In such event, the escrow agent shall return to the Buyer the purchase money held by him. If any destruction, loss or damage occurs which does not interrupt, curtail or otherwise materially affect the business, the purchase price shall be adjusted at the closing to reflect such destruction, loss or damage.

8. COVENANT NOT TO COMPETE

The Seller covenants to and with the Buyer, his successors and assigns, that for a period of five years from and after the closing she will not, directly or indirectly, either as principal, agent, manager, employee, owner, partner, shareholder, director or officer of a corporation, or otherwise, engage in any business similar to or in competition with the business hereby sold within a radius of 10 miles (16 km) of 65 Lonsdale St., Anytown, XX.

9. CONDITIONS PRECEDENT TO CLOSING

The Buyer's obligations at closing are subject to the fulfillment prior to or at closing of the following conditions:

(a) All of the Seller's representations and warranties contained in this agreement shall be true as of the time of closing.

(b) The Seller shall have complied with and performed all agreements and conditions required by this agreement to be performed or complied with prior to or at the closing.

10. CLOSING

The closing shall take place at the office of Jack D. Jack, 100 Hoh St., Anytown, XX, on December 31, 198_, at 4 p.m. At the time of said closing, all keys to the business premises, the bills of sale and other instruments of transfer shall be delivered by the Seller to the Buyer and the money of the Buyer shall be delivered to the Seller. Upon completion of the said payment and transfer, the sale shall be effective and the Buyer shall take possession of the said business.

11. INDEMNIFICATION BY THE SELLER

The Seller shall indemnify and hold the Buyer harmless against and will reimburse the Buyer on demand for any payment made by the Buyer after closing in respect to:

(a) Any liabilities and obligations of the Seller not expressly assumed by the Buyer.

(b) Any damage or deficiency resulting from misrepresentation, breach of warranty, or nonfulfillment of the terms of this agreement.

12. SELLER'S SECURITY DEPOSIT

As security for the indemnities specified in Section 11, the Seller's lawyer, Jack D. Jack, shall hold in escrow, for a period of six months from the date of closing, the sum of $10,000 which has been paid by the Buyer upon execution of this agreement. Said escrow agent shall upon application of the Buyer apply all or any part of such to reimburse the Buyer as provided in Section 11, provided the Seller shall have been given not less than ten days' notice of such application and has not questioned its propriety.

13. ARBITRATION OF DISPUTES

All controversies arising under or in connection with, or relating to any alleged breach of this agreement, shall be submited to a panel of three arbitrators. Such panel shall be composed of two members chosen by the Seller and Buyer respectively and one member selected by the arbitrators previously chosen. The findings of such arbitrators shall be conclusive and binding on the parties hereto. Such arbitrators shall also conclusively designate the party or parties to bear the expense of such determination and the amount to be borne by each.

In witness whereof the Seller and Buyer have signed this agreement.

Sally Seller
_____
Sally Seller

Billy Buyer
_____
Billy Buyer

J. M. Witness
_____
Witness

W. E. Witness
_____
Witness

November 28, 198_

14

LEASING

For the seller: *You may want to lease rather than sell some of your assets.*

If your financing plan is not feasible, or if funding for the purchase of fixed assets (land and building) that go with the business is not obtainable, you may have to consider other alternatives. One of these alternatives that minimizes the investment required, and therefore minimizes the risk, is leasing.

Most first time business owners invest far too much money in bricks and mortar (the building) when they should be leasing that asset, particularly in the early years.

It is in these early years that the risk is often the greatest, and you may not be able to afford the heavy mortgage debt load that buying a building requires. In fact, many leases can be arranged that allow you a later purchase option.

You might propose to a seller who wishes to sell the property with the business that he or she consider retaining these assets and leasing them to you.

a. LAND AND BUILDING LEASE

A lease is basically a partnership agreement between the landlord (the owner of the land and/or building) and the tenant (the operator of the building).

There is no standard form of lease agreement. Each lease agreement must be prepared by the lawyers of the two parties involved depending on the particular circumstances involved.

The agreement should cover such matters as the length of the contract (for example 5, 10, or even 20 or more years), the amount of rent and frequency of payment, the responsibility of the two parties for the maintenance of the property, and who pays which costs for items, such as major (plumbing, electrical, air conditioning) or minor (cleaning and cleaning supplies) maintenance, and other items of cost, such as building alterations, property taxes, and insurance.

An initial relatively short contract with one or more renewal options is often preferable to a long-term lease contract. Renewal options prevent you from being locked in if the business is not successful, but allow you to continue if it is a profitable enterprise.

The typical lease is generally only for the land and building, with the lessee (operator) owning the fixtures and equipment which could be offered back by the purchaser as security for the lease.

If the equipment and similar items are owned by the lessor (in which case the lease payments will generally be higher), the lease agreement should specify how frequently these items are to be replaced and at whose cost.

If the lessee owns the equipment and similar items, the lease contract should provide for the disposition of them at the end of the lease period.

The two most common arrangements are that the lessee is responsible for complete removal of such items at his or her cost, or that the lessor has the right to buy them at some stipulated value.

With any form of lease operation, it is normal for the lessee to bear the burden of any operating losses, although, depending on the lease arrangement, some of the net profit may have to be shared with the lessor under certain circumstances.

There are a variety of rental arrangement possibilities with leasing. Some of these will be discussed.

1. Fixed rental

A fixed rental arrangement calls for straight payments during the term of the lease. The payment might be a stepped one that increases, for example, year by year, during the term of the lease. However, the payments are not variable with, and do not depend on, your sales or profits.

The lease agreement will probably allow renegotiation of the fixed amount of rent during the life of the agreement, particularly if the life is for an extended number of years.

2. Variable rental

A variable rental has a fixed portion, usually at least sufficient to give the lessor cash flow to amortize loan obligations, cover expenses, and provide a return on investment.

In addition, there will be additional rent based either on your gross sales or on your net profit.

The variable rent portion gives the landlord some hedge against inflation, although there might be a ceiling rent amount stated in the contract.

3. Percentage of sales

Another possibility is for rent to be based on sales. If so, what is to be included in sales should be completely spelled out. For example, is rental income from a part of the building subleased by you to a third party to be included in sales?

Some contracts call for an increasing percentage of sales as sales increase — an escalation clause. This can be risky for you since the accelerating percentage can seriously erode normal net profit margins as sales continue to climb.

4. Percentage of net profit

With rent partly based on percentage of sales, the landlord is in a type of partnership arrangement with you. With the variable portion of rent based on net profit, this partnership becomes even more firm. The net profit must be carefully defined in the lease contract as either profit before income tax, profit before interest and tax, or profit before depreciation, interest, and tax.

In some lease contracts, to protect the landlord, the amount of certain types of expenses may be limited. For example, if your salary is not limited, you could pay yourself such an inflated amount that there would be no net profit to be shared with the landlord in the rent.

In other cases, the contract may specify a minimum expense amount that you must spend each year, for example, for advertising (so that sufficient sales and net profit are generated) or for maintenance (so that the building is kept in good condition).

5. Sale/leaseback

One other type of lease arrangement is the sale/leaseback. This occurs when a building owner sells the land to a land investor and agrees to lease it back for a number of years.

Alternatively, the owner may sell both land and the building to a property investor and contract to lease both of them back in order to be able to continue to operate the business.

When buying a business for the first time, it may also be necessary for you to seek a sale/leaseback arrangement if the seller insists on selling all the assets with the business and you cannot obtain full financing for this. You might be able to arrange in advance with a third party that, at the time the purchase of the business is concluded, the major assets will be immediately sold to that third party under a leaseback arrangement.

The sale/leaseback arrangement is also useful to a person already in business who wishes to buy another one. The cash freed up from the sale of the present land, or land and building, reduces the requirement to find financing for the new business.

6. Advantages of leasing

Some advantages of leasing are:

- Under a lease arrangement, you have the obvious advantage of not having to provide capital to buy the property. Any capital that you might have is then available for investment elsewhere.
- It also frees up your borrowing power to raise money, if required, for more critical areas of the business.
- Lease payments on a building are generally fully tax deductible.
- Also, whereas owned land is not depreciable for tax purposes, the cost of leasing land is tax deductible.

113

- You may have a purchase option at the end of the lease period when it may be desirable to buy the land and/or building and cash is available to do this.
- If and when the time comes to sell the business it may be easier to do this if there is no real estate involved.
- Finally, it may be possible to arrange a lease with rental payments adjusted to the business's seasonal cash flows, even though total annual rent would be the same amount.

7. Disadvantages of leasing

Some disadvantages of leasing are:

- One of the major disadvantages of the lease is that any capital gain in the assets accrues to the landord and not to you. In a similar way, at the expiry of the lease, the value of the future profit of the business that you have worked hard to build up does not benefit you unless the lease is renewed.
- It may also be more difficult for you to borrow money with leased premises if there are no assets (other than a lease agreement) to pledge as collateral.
- Finally, the total cash outflow in rental payments may be greater in the long run than for purchasing the property.

b. EQUIPMENT LEASE

If the business you buy needs completely new equipment and fixtures, you could also consider leasing them. Over the past few years, the leasing of shorter-life assets like equipment has become fairly common.

Most equipment leases cannot be cancelled and require you to make a series of payments whose total sum will exceed the cost of assets if purchased outright since the lessor has to make a profit on his or her investment.

Depreciation of the assets is the lessor's prerogative as owner of the assets. Maintenance is usually, but not invariably, a cost of the lessor.

Generally, the lessor owns any residual value in the assets, although contracts sometimes give you as lessee the right to purchase the assets at your option, at a specified price, at the end of the lease period. In some cases, you will also have the option to renew the lease for a specified further period.

Some suppliers of equipment will lease directly. In other cases, you will lease from a company that specializes in leasing and has bought the equipment from the supplier. The supplier may act as an intermediary in such cases.

1. Advantages of equipment leasing

Some of the advantages of equipment leasing include flexibility, 100% financing, and tax considerations.

Flexibility is considered to be an advantage because you avoid the risk of obsolescence you might have if the assets are purchased outright. However, the lessor probably considers the cost of obsolescence when the lease rates are determined.

One hundred percent financing of leased assets may be possible if there is no down payment required. One hundred percent lease financing of relatively short-lived assets (such as equipment and fixtures) also has an advantage even if you have the cash to pay for them outright. This cash is then free for investment in longer-lived assets, such as land or building, that frequently appreciate in value as time goes by. Equipment depreciates very rapidly and usually has little or no residual value.

Finally, income tax is an important consideration. Since lease payments are generally fully tax deductible, there can be an advantage in leasing. On the other hand, ownership permits deduction for income tax purposes of both depreciation and the interest expense on any debt financing of the purchase. However, what might be advantageous with one lease arrangement may be disadvantageous with another. Each situation must be considered on its own merits as far as tax implications are concerned.

15

FRANCHISING

You might also want to consider taking over an existing franchise business or buying into a franchising system and opening a new franchised outlet.

Franchising as a means for the independent entrepreneur to go into business has been booming for the last 20 years and there appears to be no immediate letup in sight.

You only need to look at popular business journals and newspaper business sections, or even in the business opportunities section of newspaper classified advertising, to see the many references made to franchised businesses.

Franchising is simply a form of distribution of a good or a service. Because of its high profile in the fast food industry, it has often been identified primarily with that type of business. But, we all use many other types of franchise goods or services each day of our lives without perhaps even realizing it.

a. A DEFINITION OF FRANCHISING

There is no commonly accepted definition of franchising that can be applied in all cases. However, in general terms, it is a method of distribution or marketing in which a company (the franchisor) grants by contract to an individual or another company (the franchisee) the right to carry on a business in a prescribed way in a particular location for a specified period.

The franchisee may be allowed to operate only one establishment, or may be given an area in which a number of franchised outlets may be operated. That area could be a city, a state or province, a major portion of the country, or indeed the whole country. For example, Wendy's in the U.S. a few years ago gave a private Canadian company the territorial rights to all of Canada for Wendy's restaurant operations.

1. Fees

For the services that it provides, the franchisor receives a fee, or royalty, usually based on gross sales, or else a fixed fee (for example, a flat monthly or annual amount, or a fixed fee based on the number of rooms in a hotel or motel franchise).

In addition, the franchisee usually has to pay a share of local, regional, or national advertising costs. Again, this advertising cost is usually a percentage of sales revenue. The fees and other costs are generally payable monthly.

For what you pay as a franchisee, you may receive business advice and counsel, financial aid (direct or indirect), market research, lease negotiation, site evaluation, building plans, training programs, national advertising, an accounting system, and an established and widely recognized name and image.

Although you must provide, or arrange for, most of the financing required, the franchisor may provide some of this initial capital. In such cases, the monthly fee will probably include an extra amount to pay back this franchisor financing, with interest.

However, even if you have to arrange for the entire financing yourself, the franchisor's credit strength and reputation can be of help in seeking a loan.

2. Requirements

As a franchisee, you will be required to maintain certain standards established by the franchisor. As an individual franchisee, you may see these standards (such as pricing policies, or the requirement to purchase products from the franchisor at a higher price than you can buy them locally) as an imposition on you as an independent entrepreneur, causing a loss of individuality.

On the other hand, you have to consider the benefits of increased business that national advertising can produce. As an individual operator, you could never afford that kind of advertising coverage.

b. ADVANTAGES OF FRANCHISING TO THE INDIVIDUAL FRANCHISEE

Some of the major advantages for the individual franchisee of taking the franchise route into business are:

- It is possible to start up as a generally independent entrepreneur but with the support of an established parent company: the franchisor. The franchisor may provide you with possible assistance in such matters as obtaining financing, site selection, building construction supervision, employee training, and support during the difficult break-in period subsequent to opening.

- As a franchisee you have the opportunity to buy into an established concept, although this, by itself, is no guarantee that you will succeed. However, the risk of failure is generally reduced. Statistics show that the independent entrepreneur opening a small business has a 20 to 30% chance of surviving the first few critical years. As a franchisee, similar statistics show there is an 80% chance of success.

- You have the ongoing backup of the franchisor who can provide assistance and help solve problems since he or she can afford to hire specialists in the head office in such areas as cost control, marketing and sales, and research and development.

- The franchisor can provide the potential for local, regional, or even national advertising (albeit at a cost to you).

- You have access to credit that you may not otherwise have. Banks and similar lending institutions are usually more willing to lend money to an entrepreneur who has the backing of a successful franchisor than they would to the completely independent entrepreneur.

- You may be able to purchase supplies at a reduced cost since the franchisor can purchase in bulk and pass the savings on to the franchisees (as much as 3 to 6% on costs may be saved this way).

- You may find an opportunity to take over a turnkey franchise operation. A turnkey operation is one where the franchisor provides you with a completely set up franchise. The franchisor provides assistance with financing; site evaluation; selection and acquisition; construction and equipping of premises; training of you and your staff; purchase of the initial inventory; management and accounting reporting systems; advertising, public relations and marketing services; and, after opening, ongoing supervision and guidance. In other words, about all you have to do is turn the key in the door and you're in business.

- You may also have an advantage if you buy a franchise already tested and successful. You will have the protection of a system already developed with a lot of start up problems already solved.

- Finally, franchising offers many of the advantages of an integrated chain business (without some of the disadvantages) because of the voluntary nature of the contract rather than central ownership.

c. DISADVANTAGES OF FRANCHISING TO THE INDIVIDUAL FRANCHISEE

Just as you must consider the advantages of the franchised form of business, so must you consider the disadvantages:

- The cost of the services provided by the franchisor comes off the top of your sales revenue and could add up to 10% or more of that revenue.

- Even though the franchise arrangement allows you to start a business that you might otherwise only be able to begin with difficulty, you will have some loss of freedom since the franchisor's standards have to be adhered to, and you may have limited scope for individual personal initiative.

- In some cases, the mark up that is added to the products that you must buy from the franchisor can increase your operating costs, particularly if an

119

equally good product could be purchased locally at a lower cost.

- Experience shows that you run some risk of not achieving the sales potential, and thus the profit, that the franchisor stated was possible when selling the franchise.

- If the franchisor operates from a jurisdiction other than the one in which you have the franchise, and his or her obligations are not fulfilled, it can be difficult, if not impossible, to seek redress.

d. LEGAL ASPECTS OF FRANCHISING

If you purchase a franchise it will likely be one that was developed in North America.

1. Disclosure in the U.S.

For several years a number of states in the U.S. have had laws requiring the franchisor to provide franchisees with a disclosure document. Their format for disclosure presentation is known as the Uniform Franchise Offering Circular (UFOC) — sometimes referred to as an offering circular or prospectus.

The rationale behind this disclosure document was the history of excesses and deceptions that some franchisors used in negotiating the sale of their franchises. Much of this deception was from franchisors overstating potential profits. In addition, hidden costs, kickbacks, the use of high profile celebrity promoters, and high pressure sales approaches have been used.

Full disclosure laws were prompted by such tactics and by the reasoning that franchise agreements are similar to securities and purchasers should have the same kind of protection provided in a stock prospectus.

2. Trade Commission Rule

One of the most important events in franchising in recent years was the introduction in 1979 by the Federal Trade Commission (FTC) of its "Trade Commission Rule" that requires all franchisors operating anywhere in the U.S. to make full disclosure to all prospective franchisees.

In effect, the rule obliges franchisors to meet certain FTC standards, such as ensuring that a reasonable basis for any claims exists, that the disclosure has been prepared in accordance with accepted accounting principles, that there is evidence to support the financial claims, and that the franchisee, among others, can see this evidence.

The FTC rule does not require the franchisor to make any claims about earnings since the franchise system may be a new one without a history of earnings or one without a central accounting system so the franchisor is unaware of the earnings of its individual franchisees. However, if the franchisor does make any claims about actual or potential earnings, these must be provided.

A copy of the proposed franchise agreement must also be provided the prospective franchisee. All these documents must be made available prior to completion of the franchise sale.

Although the FTC's disclosure rule provides a minimum federal standard throughout the country, it still allows state and local regulatory authorities to provide additional protection to potential franchisees. For example, some state laws require registration of franchisors and their franchise sales personnel, bonding and escrow, and more detailed disclosure than required by the FTC.

The FTC standards come into effect where state and local laws are inconsistent with the national standards.

It was mentioned earlier that some states allow the use of the UFOC disclosure format. To minimize compliance regulations, the FTC allows the use of the UFOC format in lieu of its own disclosure rule since UFOC provides protection to franchisees that is equal to or greater than that covered by the rule.

Note also that, whereas a disclosure statement is required by law, there is no guarantee that it has been scrutinized by any federal, state, or local regulatory agency for completeness and accuracy. Nor does it imply approval, recommendation, or endorsement by any government.

Nor does it require that you read it! The onus to do that is still on you. Take the time to do it since, despite the disclosure requirement, there are still franchisors who will attempt to ignore the law, fail to tell the truth in the disclosure document, or twist it to their advantage.

Also, to protect yourself fully, you will still have to do some further checking on your own to independently obtain information confirming what is in the disclosure documents.

3. The law in Canada

The U.S. laws and regulations governing franchise companies do not apply in Canada. Only Alberta has a Franchise Act, although Quebec may be close to implementing a similar one. The Alberta act imposes restrictions on franchisors operating in that province. The act requires disclosure of the material facts involved in operating the franchise. This requires a prospectus to be filed with the regulatory body (the Securities Commission).

A franchisor operating in other provinces in Canada does not have to file a prospectus with the provincial government so, for the most part, as a franchisee you would be on your own. However, in B.C., the Trade Practice Act does have a provision that protects the first time franchisee. The provision reads as follows: "If a person goes into a business opportunity scheme where he has to spend money and also work himself, and has no experience in that type of business, he is considered to be a consumer for the purpose of the statute."

In the U.S., the tendency is to view the franchisee as a consumer who has the right to protection against unethical franchisors. The tendency in Canada is to view the franchisee as a business person dealing with another business person on an equal basis.

4. Use a lawyer

Regardless of the situation in the U.S. or Canada, one of your best friends if you are contemplating a franchise purchase will be a lawyer. Choose one who is up to date on the legal framework of franchising. Even a reputable franchisor may have overlooked something that your lawyer (who is aware of all the local and provincial laws, such as building codes and health regulations) might notice in the contract and that should be changed.

e. IN SUMMARY

Today, it appears that everywhere you look new enterprises are opening up that offer some form of good or service that is supported by a franchised form of business, whether it be a fast food restaurant (and some not so fast food), a leisure and travel business, a retail clothing store, a real estate company, or a company specializing in tax returns.

However, do not be attracted by the bait of quick profits for minimum effort, low initial investment, and freedom to be your own boss. There are still too many entrepreneurs who, in evaluating a franchise, disregard warning lights, push aside sensible (generally negative) advice, and fail to completely examine the franchisor or the contract, even when the franchisor suggests that this be done.

Some franchisees end up being very well off, but by far the majority find themselves working harder than they anticipated under contractual arrangements that may seem harsh or restrictive since they did not provide the anticipated return on investment. Some of these entrepreneurs fail since they expected too much from too little effort on their part.

As a franchised business operator, do not mislead yourself into thinking you have complete independence. A franchisee has a degree of independence, but is controlled to a greater or lesser degree (depending on the type of franchise) by the franchisor. On the other hand, with success and with growth, it may well be that the individual who runs a successful franchise business will eventually become a franchisor, selling franchises to others who wish to become franchisees.

For more detailed information on franchising, see *Franchising in the U.S.* or *Franchising in Canada*, also published by Self-Counsel Press.

16
SELLING YOUR BUSINESS: GETTING STARTED

For the seller: *The next two chapters deal specifically with items of concern to you.*

Each buyer needs a seller, and a buyer today will probably eventually be a seller also. Just as sellers can benefit from knowing what a buyer is looking for, seeing a business through a seller's eyes may give the buyer an edge.

In simple terms, you could say that selling a business is simply the reverse of buying — that what is advantageous to the buyer must be disadvantageous to the seller, and vice versa. Thus, if you know all about buying a business, you must therefore know all about selling one. But it is not quite that simple.

a. SIX BLIND BEGGARS

You have no doubt heard the story of the six blind beggars who learned that an elephant was going to be passing by. Since they were not familiar with elephants, other than by name, they perceived this as an opportunity to find out all about elephants.

As the elephant passed by, the first beggar touched it on its huge side and decided it was just like a wall.

The second blind beggar managed to grab the elephant's trunk and declared the elephant to be a large snake.

The third beggar happened to grasp one of the elephant's huge legs while the elephant had stopped and stated that the elephant was like a tree.

The fourth one clutched a tusk and announced that, because it was smooth and sharp, an elephant was just like a spear.

The fifth grasped upwards and held on to the elephant's ear and decided, since the ear was flapping, that the elephant was like a fan.

Finally, the last blind beggar, being slower than the others, could only hang on to the elephant's tail as the animal walked by. Scornful of the others, he declared the elephant to be just another piece of rope.

The elephant and its driver continued on their way while the six blind beggars discussed, argued, and came to no agreement as to what an elephant was. But then, how could they?

The only person who really knew was the driver, since he was on top of the whole situation. . . .

And so it is with your company. You are the driver. Outsiders cannot see as you can, and it is up to you to describe your business to them, if you wish to sell it, so they can see it as well as you.

b. SELLING PLAN

You have to develop and then follow through on a selling plan that will result in the successful completion of a satisfactory sales agreement. This plan should include the preparation of at least the following:

- an information package or brochure
- a list of potential purchasers
- a set of procedures you will use to make contact with those potential purchasers
- a set of procedures to discover the motivation of potential purchasers
- an attitude that you will stick to throughout your business selling effort

c. DESCRIBING YOUR BUSINESS

A good written narrative, without being too wordy, describing the history of your business will be of help in explaining how your company started, where it has been, and where it could go. This narrative should be honest, since serious buyers will soon recognize deception.

Your narrative should describe such items as the background of the present owners, what their education and experience was prior to starting or taking over the business, the size of the business when it was started, what its main products or services were initially, and how these were added to over the years, who its major customers were and are, how many employees it began with and has now, any changes in management in recent years, and whether any of the present owners and key management people wish to stay with the business after its sale.

Of course the prospective purchasers could find out this information by asking questions, but it is certainly more effective to have this information prepared in written form. It saves them time, indicates your businesslike approach to selling the business, and reflects the manner in which you have been running the business.

1. Summary sheet

A summary sheet about the sale to accompany the background narrative would also be helpful. For example, a summary sheet might read as follows:

SUMMARY SHEET

The business for sale is a distributing company owning its own premises. It sells copying machines to small- and medium-sized businesses. The present owner is selling in order to retire from active business. Present annual sales volume is $750,000. This sales volume has been growing at 7 to 8% per year for the past five years. Pretax profits, after deduction of the owner's annual salary of $30,000, have averaged $33,000 for the past three years. The business has suffered no loss years since it began seven years ago. Audited statements are available on request by serious purchasers. The business has five full-time employees and hires part-time sales and office people as required. Asking price for the business is $300,000 cash, although the owner is willing to consider offers and the assumption of a mortgage on the building. Sale is direct by the owner — no broker or other intermediary is involved. For further information contact the owner at (600) 666-6666.

---

d. DO YOU REALLY WANT TO SELL?

At this point you have prepared your narrative and some basic statistical information on a summary sheet for prospective purchasers. Now you must make a final decision about whether you really want to sell.

It is often said that there are two happy days in the life of a person who owns his or her own business — the day that it is purchased and the day that it is sold. Since you've already lost the first happy day, are you now prepared to lose the second?

You know that you have to sell to a buyer who values the business as much as you do, and for this reason selling can be more difficult than buying, particularly if you have enjoyed the business you have lived with and run profitably.

1. Changing commitment

Selling your business is a very personal matter and it takes time to arrive at a satisfactory sale. This time could vary from a month to a year or more, and if you continue to operate the business while trying to sell it, which would be the normal situation, a number of things can happen during the selling period.

Once you have decided to sell, your commitment to the business will change. So will the commitment of your employees. The momentum of the business can decline since an attitude of uncertainty in both you and your employees will prevail. This can, in fact, cause a deterioration in employee relations, which can be reflected in productivity and sales — and the longer the sale takes, the more severe this deterioration can be. You may have to work hard to ensure that it does not cause a decrease in the perceived value of your business to a prospective purchaser.

2. Detailed sales list

At this point, having confirmed in your mind that you do wish to sell the business, you are ready to prepare a more detailed checklist (for serious purchasers).

This checklist should include enough information to attract potential purchasers and spark their interest. Only enough data should be presented so that serious potential purchasers can decide either to seek further information from you or else to proceed no further. If this checklist is professionally presented, it puts you in early command of the situation and will establish the tone for further negotiation. Real estate firms or business brokers, if you are going to use them in your sales strategy, can be very helpful in preparing this checklist. They know from experience what type of information prospective purchasers need. The pros and cons of using a broker will be discussed in the next chapter.

Your checklist could include the following:

- Exact location of the business and physical description of the property
- Size of land and building area
- Age of building and type of construction
- Annual property operation costs such as taxes, insurance and maintenance
- Leasehold information — what property or equipment is leased and lease expiry and renewal information
- Annual rent on any leased premises
- Geographic trading area and list of suppliers
- Present and anticipated competitors — who they are, how strong they are, how long they have been in business, and even what their sales strategies are
- List of present suppliers and terms of any purchase contracts
- List of current customers/clients and ageing list of receivables
- Inventory information — how valued and present value
- List of equipment and related depreciation schedules
- Number of employees, union involvement, date of contract termination

- Major products sold, how sold, and commission rates, if goods sold on commission

- Historic sales figures for at least the last three years, assuming you have owned the business for that long.

- Terms of the sale: cash down payment expected and other related information. However, at this point you should not allocate the sale price among the assets (see chapter 13 for a discussion of this) since it might confuse potential purchasers.

- If there are any major problems with your business you should include them in the checklist. This does not mean listing every single problem, but if there is something a potential purchaser should know, it is better to raise it now rather than have the purchaser later believe you were trying to mislead him or her. You must maintain your credibility.

3. Preparing a brochure

Some businesses for sale present their information in the form of a pamphlet or brochure. In such cases, the fact sheet information can be expanded. In addition, if space permits, one or two photographs of the operation, both outside and inside, would be useful. If appropriate, further photographs of the immediate surroundings could be added. For example, if your business is in a shopping center, include a photograph or two of the center surroundings. Supplement the photos with a written summary of the surroundings emphasizing details such as number and type of other businesses, residential make-up of the neighborhood, and any unique attractions. This section could include a map of the surroundings showing the specific location of your business.

One other item to consider including is the name of the person potential purchasers can contact for further information. This may mean providing a name and telephone number apart from that of the business or you might want to use a telephone answering service.

4. Sprucing up your image

Make your business as physically attractive as possible. You need to put your best foot forward. This does not mean major renovations, but perhaps a coat of paint, both inside and out, would help. First impressions are important and it would be a shame to lose a good prospect because your business has an untidy, cluttered apearance. It may also show employees that you are still concerned about the business.

e. FINDING A BUYER

People who are prospective purchasers will be hard-working people like yourself who are cautious and want to know all the facts before making decisions. They will want to deal with you on the basis of a fair price and will not want to waste their time trying to talk you into selling your business if you show any reluctance. A serious buyer wants a serious seller.

However, approaching a buyer is a delicate matter. Initially, you have the advantage since you have probably established a price and have the facts to support it. But, if you take the initiative to approach a buyer, you are at a disadvantage. You need to indicate your business's availability without making it too obvious you are anxious to sell.

Another problem is to find good buyers. One way to do this is to spread the word through all the channels listed in chapter 5 that a prospective purchaser might use to seek a business that is for sale.

In addition to those channels, consider the following possibilities:

- Former employers. If you have previously worked for companies in the same line of business as the one you now wish to sell, former employers might be willing to expand their own business by buying you out.

- Present and former employees. These could be excellent prospects since they know your business and, if they are anxious to start up for themselves, buying a business they are familiar with will give them a greater sense of security. In addition, you will know their capabilities; if they would be good business operators, this helps ensure their ability to pay you.

- Business suppliers. Sometimes suppliers may be interested in purchasing a business if it will provide them economies of scale by integrating it with their own.
- Competitors. Competitors may be interested in buying your business in order to reduce competition to themselves, or to convert it to a business more compatible with their own, or to expand their own operations.
- The classified section. Check the classified section of your local newspaper to see if anyone has advertised seeking business opportunities.

Selling a business is no different from selling any other product. If you have been good at selling your business's products, then you should have no difficulty finding prospective buyers.

1. Contacting potential purchasers

There are various ways to contact prospective purchasers. Start with people you know. This can be done by telephone or mail. This personal contact can be advantageous for several reasons. First, a personal contact can add an air of integrity to negotiations. Second, personal contacts already know something about your capabilities, and you will probably know something about their operating and financial capabilities, and even about their investment objectives. Third, these potential purchasers can discuss the situation directly with you. This will reduce the opportunity for misunderstanding that can sometimes arise if discussions are held through a third party such as a business broker. Fourth, even if these prospects are not interested in buying your business, they may lead you to other prospects who are.

Personal contacts with people you know or whom you have been referred to, or to whom you have sent a mailing and followed up with a telephone call, are preferable to the alternative: advertising.

2. Advertising

One of the more direct ways to find buyers is to advertise. For a small business, the best advertising medium is the business opportunities section of your local major newspaper.

The wording of your advertisement is important. Business buyers are no different than anyone else — they are looking for a good opportunity at a better than normal price, preferably with no money down! You are looking for a serious buyer who can come up with some cash and afford to buy your business.

Your advertisement must show that your business is profitable and will appeal to the serious buyer. Advertisements can be kept simple but must detail the important relevant facts. A typical advertisement might read as follows:

BUSINESS FOR SALE. Clothing store for sale. Annual sales $150,000. Twelve years in excellent location near downtown Anytown. Steady return clientele. Selling price will yield excellent return on investment. Sale terms open to negotiation. Phone (600) 666-6666.

---

3. Strange offers

Advertising, particularly in local newspapers, will elicit all kinds of responses. These responses could be from applicants for jobs, sales agents wanting a listing, competitors trying to find out more about your business to help them with their own operations, consultants offering to help you (for a fee or commission!), and even suppliers wanting to find out if they should keep supplying you if you intend to go out of business. You will receive many calls from people who tell you they have just won a lottery and will offer you all kinds of interesting deals if you will just cut your selling price in half.

You will receive offers from people who will agree to take over your business and run it more profitably than you have been able to and pay you out of those anticipated additional profits (with nothing down).

Others will offer to buy your inventory from you if you will let them occupy the premises for nothing. They might even suggest you pay them for taking over your business problems. These are the "tire kickers" who really aren't to be taken too seriously but that you have to endure until you can get rid of them.

You will also get Sunday shoppers who are similar to the people who regularly visit every "open house" in the neighborhood with no intention of buying. You will also get the jawboners who are simply curious and will also just waste your time.

You will also have people who want to either take over your business on a management contract basis, or on a lease arrangement with an option to buy if things work out. In these two situations you are, of course, not free of the business. You should only follow through on such offers if they are part of your strategy; otherwise, don't waste your time since you will continue to assume the business risk while leaving the day-to-day operations in the hands of someone else.

In particular, beware of the person who offers to take over your operation for six months to obtain experience with it, at the end of which period negotiations can begin. You could end up with a lot of grief, including unnecessary bills and negative goodwill. To counter such an offer you should first ask for a nonrefundable deposit in the event the sale does not go through, and second state that the sale price at the end of that time will be based on a non-negotiable professional appraisal of the business's worth.

It is up to you to spot the serious purchasers, such as the retired long-time business executive who wants a new challenge in life, or the owner of a present business who wants a change of opportunity. These people are the ones you must sit down with and gradually work out a deal that is reasonable for both parties.

4. Finder's fees

You will probably also receive responses from those who offer to introduce you to a potential purchaser for a fee. This could be legitimate. Normally, such a fee is a fixed amount but, where the law allows (such as in the case of a licensed real estate broker), it could be a percentage of the sale price. Beware of anyone who might be a potential purchaser's friend or relative who is simply fronting for him or her with the fee split between them. To the purchaser this reduces the purchase cost of the business by the amount of fee received.

On the other hand, in your advertising, you might state that you are willing to pay a finder's fee. However, if you make this offer, pay the fee only after the sale is finalized and, for protection, detail the facts about the finder's fee in the sales contract. Do not have a separate finder's fee agreement stating that you will pay the fee to a named person when he or she simply produces a prospective purchaser.

5. Checking out prospective purchasers

Once you have found a serious purchaser, you have to do some checking. You can never do too much of that.

References are important, particularly those from reputable, well-known financial institutions that the prospective purchaser has done business with.

You need these references to determine the purchaser's personal background, business success, financial success, names of other business associates, and possibly even educational background. Use references for further references — you cannot do too much checking in this regard.

Even though the prospective purchaser's bank may be reticent about giving out financial information about its clients, you may be able to use your own bank to run a credit check on him or her. In particular try to find out the purchaser's net worth or obtain a personal financial statement.

Do not give away too much information about your business, particularly matters of a financial nature, until you have checked the buyer's references from at least two professional people (banker, accountant, lawyer). However, do not hesitate to give out narrative sheets, summary sheets, and detailed sales lists described earlier in this chapter.

6. Purchaser motivation

It is important to discover as much as you can about potential purchasers. Reference checks can provide some information but often do not disclose other important facts such as the purchaser's motivation for buying your business. If you know "why," you can use this to advantage in your negotiations. For example, if a competitor wishes to take over your operation in order to expand his or her market share, you can use this information to your advantage. Similarly, if a developer is buying up land around your business to put up a shopping mall and needs your property to complete the land package, you have a lever to maximize the selling price. Finding out the "why" often requires some leg-work, but it can be profitable.

7. Compromises

In your negotiations, you must establish in advance the compromises or trade-offs you will accept to conclude the sale. For example, you must present information to potential purchasers to attract their attention, but not disclose so much about your business that it could harm negotiations.

Your information sheet or brochure is only the first round in information disclosure. Further information should be disclosed only to serious purchasers. Don't waste your time providing more information to other types of prospects. Serious purchasers are those who do any or all of the following:

- Provide you with a personal resume
- Disclose information about themselves in the form of a personal financial statement showing their net worth
- Provide you with a banker's letter of credit demonstrating ability to pay
- Make a firm purchase offer along with a nonrefundable deposit

However, even with serious purchasers, don't get carried away about the things of value in your business. The potential purchaser might feel compelled to find faults with your operations that he or she can use as bargaining tools.

8. Disclosing problems

A serious dilemma for the seller is whether or not, when negotiations do become intense, to disclose all the problems that go along with your business. An astute purchaser will notice serious problems, and if you do not disclose them, the purchaser may wonder what else you are trying to hide. The dilemma comes not from obvious problems that you have learned to overcome and that you have used as opportunities for business success, but from problems that might be seen as serious flaws from a buyer's perspective. It's a fine line to tread and sellers are often guided by the phrase "caveat emptor" — let the buyer beware. But there can be legal risks in this as a result of non-disclosure of serious problems that mislead the purchaser. There is really no need to bring small problems into the discussions since they are part of every business, and wasting time on them may tend only to muddy the waters.

9. Don't abandon ship

Once the sales decision has been made, do not succumb to the temptation to abandon ship. This could cause the business to run down and will jeopardize a sale.

17

FINALIZING THE SALE PRICE AND USING AGENTS

a. FINALIZING THE PRICE

It is common practice for sellers to ask for more than they expect the business to sell for and for prospective purchasers to offer less than they expect to pay. This makes negotiating an inevitable part of the buying/selling process. About the only time it does not occur is when a major corporation approaches a small business owner with an offer. In those cases, it is common for that offer to be the corporation's best price, with no room to negotiate. A business operator wishing to sell a business in such circumstances should recognize this situation and accept it for what it is. Usually, the advantage to you as seller is that the sale will be all cash, leaving you at no risk from continued financial investment.

Don't be too anxious to sell to the first apparently reputable purchaser. Promises of major cash backup may be nothing more than promises. At the first sign of trouble, or lack of financial backup, do not be afraid to discontinue negotiations. There will be other buyers if your price is reasonable, and obtaining a reasonable assured price is better than selling for a high price that the purchaser cannot afford.

One of the major causes of failure for a new business is lack of working capital to carry the business until it is successful. But the same is true of the sale of a business. If it is sold to a purchaser for a low down payment borrowed with a promissory note for the balance at today's high interest rates, you may be running the greater risk.

You must receive an adequate down payment that shows a commitment by the purchaser, or sell to a purchaser who can show concrete evidence of financial support from a financial institution or from other resources.

1. Help in securing financing

In some cases, the potential buyer will ask for help in securing financing. There are risks in this, particularly if financing is obtained from a lender who knows you and not the purchaser. Your name lends credibility. The risk is that, if the purchaser is unable to later make payments toward these financial commitments, your credibility may be damaged on future business ventures of your own. This risk is compounded if the lender will lend only on the condition that you retain a financial interest in the business. This may be acceptable to you, but you should then ask two questions:

(a) If the purchaser fails to meet his or her obligation, what are your additional financial responsibilities?

(b) As the former business owner now taking a back-seat, can you stand back and accept someone else operating your business?

2. Carryback financing

In establishing a sales price for the business the seller must make compromises. Generally, the higher the selling price the greater may be the sacrifice in terms and conditions of sale. For example, the higher the price, the longer the list of conditions the purchaser may want you to accept.

One of those conditions may be that you accept less than full cash for the business; you carry the balance (by way of a promissory note, mortgage, or some other financial instrument) and are paid off over time (also referred to as carryback financing). It is sometimes very difficult to sell a business without taking on the burden of carryback financing. Note also that if you do take on this burden, you are unlikely to receive any security for your continued investment in the business other than the business itself. Carryback financing could put you in the situation of being a second, or even third, mortgage holder on the business's land, building, and equipment. And if you do take a secondary or lower position, your periodic payments from the purchaser may have to be reduced in order not to burden the purchaser with too heavy a financial load. You would be extremely anxious to sell your business to accept this type of financial arrangement.

On the other hand, if you are to take over carryback financing, you do not want to make the periodic payments so high that you are constantly fighting with late payments or with the purchaser's desire to re-negotiate repayment terms.

The purchaser may even propose that your carryback financing periodic payments vary with sales volume, net profit, or some other operating measure. If you accept this arrangement, it adds an extra dimension to your responsibility since you must continually monitor, or even audit, the purchaser's income statements to ensure that the loan payments made are in accordance with the agreed terms. Also, what happens if the purchaser, unable to succeed in the business, simply closes the door? You should address this possibility in the buy/sell contract to ensure you are not abandoned.

If the purchaser's operation of the business is not successful, partly because the purchase price was too high to make the operation financially viable, you may be required to foreclose on the business. The down payment you received may make this more acceptable, but the fact is that now the business has not been sold by you, and you may be forced to operate, then try to sell again, a business that has been badly run down by the unsuccessful purchaser.

It may be better to accept a lower selling price to avoid the risk. Set priorities and consider alternative trade-offs in your selling strategy.

3. Trade-offs

An important factor in considering trade-offs is how much you will lower your price in order to be cashed out — that is, to be fully paid for the business with no further financial interest in it.

To cash out you might have to discount or lower your selling price considerably. If you do this, you should insist that a contract be signed without delay and that the sale is made on an "as is" basis. This means that the purchaser is willing to take some risk for the lowered price.

4. Low-ball offers

You may receive what is known as a low-ball offer — one that is considerably less than the business is truly worth. An immediate reaction is to reject such an offer. That might not be the best idea, particularly if the offer is signed and includes a non-refundable deposit with the balance of the sale price paid fully in cash on closing.

What you have to consider is that even though such an offer may be very low, there is always the possibility it is the only one you will receive and if you turn it down you could end up eventually giving away the business for even less than the firm offer. With a low-ball offer there is the risk that if you delay too long, either the prospective purchaser could withdraw the offer at any time after advising you, or that it will be no longer valid if you counter with a higher price than that offered.

Of course, if your business is presently losing money, you might be quite happy to immediately accept a low-ball offer, even if it represents a "steal" to the purchaser, since it will end your cash outflow. If you don't accept the offer you are simply perpetuating your losses.

5. Alternatives

If your business is successful, but you receive no cash offers for its sale, you might consider alternatives. For example, you might try to sell part of the business to a partner who can inject new and profitable ideas into its operation.

6. Selling shares

Another alternative is to sell some of the shares if your business is incorporated, or incorporate it and then sell some shares. In this way you can retain a management position and give the new shareholders an option to buy further shares as profits allow until they eventually take over the entire company. Even if those first share purchasers don't want to expand their shareholdings in the company, you may be able to sell shares to third parties.

Selling shares to employees who can be groomed to be eventual managers, operators, and owners is a useful way to go particularly if an outright sale of the business is not possible.

7. Accepting shares

You may receive an offer from a large corporation (such as a supplier) to accept shares in that corporation for the value of the business. This might be acceptable if the shares have an established market and can be easily traded.

If the offer is for preferred stock, you would be even better off since preferred stock pays dividends prior to common stock, and these dividends are usually cumulative. This means that if dividends are not paid in a particular year you are still entitled to them before common stockholders receive any future dividends, although there is no legal obligation for the corporation to ever pay those dividends if it does not wish to or does not have the cash to do so. However, there is no guaranteed security in either common or preferred shares should the corporation go into bankruptcy or liquidation at some future time. In other words, there is a risk.

A major advantage in accepting stock is that you can normally defer capital gains tax liability, whereas if you receive cash for your business and a capital gains tax is payable, it is due on filing your next tax return.

If the shares offered for your business are in a corporation in which stock is not commonly traded, then you should probably not even consider the offer since your risk is too high.

8. Accepting property

An offer may take the form of trading your business for a piece of property. This concept is similar to accepting shares. Again there may be tax advantages to doing this.

However, unlike easily marketable shares, property (land and/or buildings) might be quite difficult, and even quite expensive, to convert to cash when you want to do so.

9. Management contracts and leases

I suggested earlier that you not consider an offer from someone wanting to take over on a management contract with an option to buy, or wanting an offer to lease with an option to buy. Slightly more advantageous is a lease/purchase arrangement. This is where an actual sale contract is signed but its implementation is deferred for 12 months for example. Before or at the end of that period the lessee must purchase at the price, and under the terms and conditions, stated in the contract.

10. Income tax advice

Before any sale is concluded, consult a professional tax adviser. As a business operator it is unlikely that you are familiar with the tax implications of a buy/sell contract. Your agent, if you have one, is likely to be familiar with some of the tax implications, but not enough to give you detailed tax advice. The price you pay for professional advice can be well worth it considering the tax savings a professional can find you.

11. Sunk costs

There are costs attached to selling a business, apart from the cost of your time. For example, there are costs attached to running credit checks on potential buyers, or in using professionals to help finalize the sale. These are necessary and trying to do without them can be more costly in the long run if, as a result, the sale does not go through.

On the other hand, you may spend a great deal of time and money trying to finalize a sale that, during its later stages, does not seem to be quite right. But the temptation may be there to finalize it anyway since you have sunk so much money into the deal already. Common sense must prevail and if the "deal" is not right it should not be finalized.

142

12. In summary

It should be quite clear to you now that when you perceive the value of your business to be is not necessarily what you will sell it for.

The buyer has a price based on perceived value, and your price must be no more than the buyer's perceived value for the sale to occur. Sometimes only skillful negotiation on your part can raise the prospective purchaser's perception of value.

Questions such as the following must be considered in your negotiating:

- How sincere are you in wishing to sell your business?
- Must you sell at below your perceived value because of cash problems, ill health, or some other reason?
- How badly does the buyer want to buy into your type of business?
- How badly does the buyer want to buy your specific business?

In other words, know as much about your own motives as well as the buyer's since these are critical elements in the negotiating process.

Finally, be careful, be suspicious if necessary, but be thorough and use your judgment.

b. USING AGENTS

Now we come to the question of whether or not to use a real estate firm or business broker to help you sell your business. If you do contact such a company to act on your behalf, you must be prepared to list your business with it so that it can earn a commission from the sale. A listing agreement will detail the commission you agree to pay for the agent's sales efforts. It will also include many of the details that a potential purchaser will need to know, such as the information checklist outlined in chapter 16.

Before you use a broker or sales agent you need to weigh the following advantages and disadvantages.

1. Advantages

- Agents (particularly those attached to business brokerage firms) are in the business of selling businesses. This is their specialty. You may know how to successfully operate your business, but you may not know how to sell it.

- Agents can usually help you establish a realistic sale price for your business. You may tend to set too high a price because of emotional or financial involvement. Agents can compare your business with similar ones that have been bought and sold and may have access to financial information about other businesses that you do not have.

- Agents generally have more contacts than you have. This is particularly true with companies that specialize in business brokerage (that compared to real estate firms do not necessarily specialize in business sales). sales).

- They can act as a buffer between you and the "tire kickers." They can fend off questions that are irrelevant, handle phone calls, and even act as an emotional screen between you and potential purchasers. This alone can be a service worth paying for.

- Agents can screen potential purchasers. They can sort out the prospects who appear to have the financial, operational, or other abilities needed to take over your business. They can run credit checks and check references. In other words, they can sort out the prospects from the suspects.

- They can usually do a better job of keeping quiet about the fact that your business is for sale. If you advertise directly (without an agent), suppliers, employees, competitors, and others will find out your business is for sale before the time is really right for them to know. For example, employee morale can decline if the word is out too soon, suppliers may begin to worry that your creditworthiness is slipping, and so forth.

- Agents can often steer potential purchasers to necessary financing since they have dealt with certain

financial institutions in previous buy/sell transactions.
- They can assist purchasers in applying for and obtaining all necessary operating licenses, permits, and similar documents.
- Agents attached to larger business brokerage houses
may be able to put together an investment group that
may be willing to buy your business from their business acquaintances.

2. Disadvantages

- There is a cost attached to an agent's services. This
cost can be as high as 10% of the business's sale price,
so on a $500,000 sale price this represents $50,000.
Would you spend this much trying to sell the business
yourself, even if it took much longer to do it and
involved a great deal of your time?
- Even though you are paying for an agent's time and
services, there may not be a meaningful reduction in
the demands on your time. You still need to concen-
trate on the operation of your business to ensure it
does not run down, but the use of an agent doesn't
always gives you the freedom to do this.
- If your business is fairly large, the agent may not be
able to cope with it. Most agents deal with entrepre-
neurial purchasers. If you need to sell your business to
a larger firm, the agent may not have contacts in those
areas beyond those you have yourself.
- Local laws in your area may require an agent to present all purchase offers, regardless of the agent's opinion of their value. This means that the value of an
agent as a buffer to screen out offers is lost.
- Local laws may stipulate that only certain licensed
agents may receive a percentage fee on the sale price
of your business. Any other type of agent can earn
only a fixed fee. This may discourage a fixed fee agent
from obtaining the best price possible for your
business.

- If your commission or fee is payable only when the sale is concluded, and your business is not a very large one, the agent may pay less attention to your sale than to a larger one that comes along offering a greater incentive.

- If an agent is not very good, he or she can be motivated to sell your business at any price in order to earn a fee or commission, particularly if the income to that agent is to be paid only at the conclusion of the sale.

- An agent may get into a conflict of interest situation. When you employ an agent he or she has a legal and financial obligation to you. However, sometimes potential purchasers will ask the agent for advice and the agent may give advice that is not advantageous to you.

- Another conflict of interest situation for an agent is that a buyer of your business is a future potential seller for the agent. If the agent does a good job for the buyer, and possibly a worse job for you, that could represent a potential future commission to the agent.

- Agents sometimes use businesses primarily to generate a list of contacts for other similar businesses that he or she may have listed for sale, particularly if he or she sees that it may be difficult to sell.

- There may be financial implications in an agent's listing agreement that you do not fully understand. For example, most listings are for a fixed period of time, such as 90 days, after which the listing is either renewed or expires. However, many contracts state that if a sale is concluded after expiry as a result of earlier efforts that can be traced to that agent, then the commission is still payable.

- Most listing contracts require the agent to obtain an offer, or offers, at the price, terms, and conditions stipulated in the listing agreement. If an agent brings you a bona fide offer at the price, terms, and conditions agreed to, then you are normally legally obligated to pay the commission, even if the sale is never finalized because you do not accept the offer.

- Finally, in order to do the best job for you, an agent must be provided with a great deal of confidential information about your business — information that you may be reluctant to have made known, but without which the agent's chances of selling your business are considerably reduced.

3. Buyer's agent

It is likely that during the process of trying to sell your business you, or your agent if you are using one, will come up against a prospect who is also represented by an agent. If two agents are involved, they can negotiate on behalf of each of their respective parties. The only difficulty with this is that you are then dealing with a third party and this may prevent you from learning as much about the potential purchaser and the use to which your business will be put.

Finally, note that if you do not have an agent (in order to save the commission cost) and are dealing directly with the buyer's agent, that agent will probably want you to sign a listing agreement. That means you will pay a commission anyway if that agent sells the business. In such a case, if the agent has a suitable prospective customer, make sure the listing agreement is valid only for that particular purchaser. This will help ensure that an agent does not insist that a purchaser is available merely to obtain your sales listing.

APPENDIX

SAMPLE FINANCING PROPOSAL

Personal resume

Name	Resta Rant
Address	#1201 - 1855 Columbia Anytown, Anywhere
Telephone	234-5678
Personal	Born September 15, 1958 Marital status: single
Education	Completed high school in Anytown
	Received Hotel/Restaurant Management diploma at Community College, Anytown, 1977
	Since then I have taken some other specialized night courses in marketing and public relations at the college.
Employment/ business experience	Worked as waitress part-time while going to high school and attending college.
	From 1977 to 1984 worked in various restaurants as waitress, cashier and hostess.
	Since 1984 have been the manager of the Ritz Restaurant in Anytown.
	The present owner of the Ritz Restaurant assumed ownership 4 years ago when the restaurant was losing money. During this period this situation was turned around and for the past 3 years the restaurant has made a steady annual profit.

Business to be purchased

My plan is to purchase the Ritz Restaurant from the present owner who wishes to retire. The restaurant is located in the National Bank Building in Anytown and has a steady clientele, primarily from adjacent businesses and shops, and is open 6 days a week.

The income statements appended show that sales and profits have been steady year round for the past 3 years. Sales average $30,000 a month and net profit is $1,500 a month.

With my experience as manager of that restaurant for the past 4 years I am sure I can continue to operate it successfully.

Sales plan

My sales plan is to refurbish the restaurant and replace the 10 seat counter area with a liquor service bar.

In addition I propose to obtain a liquor license for the restaurant. I have discussed this possibility with the liquor authorities and they assure me that this should not be a problem.

With this license I project that I can increase sales (despite the loss of the 10 counter seats) by at least 10% or $3,000 a month, and increase net profit by $1,000 a month to $2,500.

Personal financial information

This personal financial information is relevant as at December 31, 1988.

Assets:
Bank accounts	
— checking	$ 300
— savings	2,200
Government bonds	15,000
Stocks — market value	3,800
Automobile	2,700
Real estate — condominium	105,000
Total assets	$129,000

Liabilities:
Accounts payable — charge accounts	700
Mortgage payable (condominium)	79,000
Installment account (auto)	2,200
Other liabilities	0
Total liabilities	$81,900
Net worth	$47,100

References

Banks:
1. National Bank
   Main Branch
   Anytown
   (checking account #7-456890 and
   savings account 64-102076)

2. Savers Credit Union
   Main Branch
   Anytown
   (mortgage records)

Lawyer:
Sol Iciter
Beagle, Legal, & Iciter
#107 - 455 Humber St.
Anytown
(434-5736)

Accountant:
Charlene Counter
Counter & Total
#512 - 1040 Broadway
Anytown
(732-1611)

Financial projections

Total purchase price of the business will be as follows:

Inventory	$ 2,000
Equipment and fixtures	46,000
Goodwill	20,000
Refurbishing and bar (supplier quoted price)	17,000
Total	$85,000

In addition I estimate I will need $5,000 for working capital for a total investment needed of $90,000.

The plan for financing this $90,000 investment is as follows:

Personal savings (equity investment) from cash and by selling stocks and bonds	$18,000
Bank loan for balance	72,000
Total	$90,000

The bank loan will be repayable in equal monthly installments of principal and interest over 3 years. Given current interest rates the monthly total repayment amount for principal and interest is calculated to be $2,500.

Income statement

Given the appended income statements from the previous owner, and the increased sales anticipated, the forecast monthly income statement is as follows:

Sales:		
food	$30,000	
beverage	3,000	
		$33,000
Cost of sales:		
food	$12,000	
beverage	900	
		12,900
Gross profit		$20,100
Expenses:		
Payroll	$10,400	
Employee benefits	2,100	
Laundry	200	
China, glass, silver	100	
Supplies	200	
Miscellaneous	200	
Advertising	200	
Utilities	300	
Management salary	1,800	
Office	500	
Rent	600	
Insurance	100	
Interest	700	
Depreciation	200	
		$17,600
Net profit		$ 2,500

Cash flow

The monthly cash flow from the business will be:

Monthly net profit	$2,500
Add back depreciation	200
	$2,700
Deduct principal repayments	1,900
Net cash flow	$ 800

This net cash flow shows a relatively high margin of safety.

Security offered

The following security is offered:

1. Personal guarantee
2. Chattel mortgage on furniture and equipment.
3. Lease agreement (present lease has 2 more years to run). I have discussed extensions to this lease and the landlord agrees that, if financing can be acquired, he would be prepared to renegotiate the lease for a 5 year period effective immediately, with a further 5 year renewal option. Rent payments will be as at present, with rent tied to the CPI for inflationary purposes at the start of each new year. The landlord can be contacted to confirm this arrangement:

   Mr. John Lessor
   Ipso Investments
   #307 - 4551 Main St.
   Anytown
   684-4685
4. Additional security can be offered, if necessary, by way of a 2nd mortgage (trust deed) on the condominium.

CANADIAN
ORDER FORM
SELF-COUNSEL SERIES

NATIONAL TITLES

Asking Questions	7.95
Assertiveness for Managers	9.95
Basic Accounting	6.95
Be a Better Manager	8.95
Best Ways to Make Money	5.95
Better Book for Getting Hired	9.95
Between the Sexes	8.95
Business Etiquette Today	7.95
Business Guide to Effective Speaking	6.95
Business Guide to Profitable Customer Relations	
Business Writing Workbook	9.95
Buying and Selling a Small Business	6.95
Civil Rights	8.95
Complete Guide to Home Contracting	19.95
Credit, Debt, and Bankruptcy	7.95
Criminal Procedure in Canada	16.95
Death in the Family	8.95
Design Your Own Logo	9.95
Editing Your Newsletter	14.95
Entrepreneur's Self-Assessment Guide	9.95
Environmental Law	8.95
Family Ties That Bind	7.95
Federal Incorporation and Business Guide	14.95
Financial Control for the Small Business	6.95
Financial Freedom on $5 a Day	7.95
For Sale By Owner	6.95
Forming and Managing a Non-Profit Organization in Canada	12.95
Franchising in Canada	6.95
Fundraising	5.50
Getting Elected	8.95
Getting Started	10.95
How to Advertise	7.95
How You Too Can Make a Million in the Mail Order Busiess	9.95
Immigrating to Canada	14.95
Immigrating to the U.S.A.	14.95
Keyboarding for Kids	7.95
Landlording in Canada	14.95
Learn to Type Fast	11.50
Managing Stress	7.95
Marketing Your Product	12.95
Marketing Your Service	12.95
Media Law Handbook	6.50
Medical Law Handbook	6.95
Mike Grenby's Tax Tips	6.95
Mobile Retirement Handbook	9.95
Mortgages & Foreclosure	7.95
A Nanny For Your Child	7.95
Newcomer's Guide to the U.S.A.	12.95
Parent's Guide to Understanding Teenagers and Suicide	
Patent Your Own Invention	21.95
Planning for Financial Independence	11.95
Practical Guide to Financial Management	6.95
Practical Time Management	6.95
Radio Documentary Handbook	8.95
Ready-to-Use Business Forms	9.95
Retirement Guide for Canadians	9.95
Selling Strategies for Service Businesses	
Small Business Guide to Employee Selection	6.95
Sport and Recreation Law in Canada	
Start and Run a Profitable Beauty Salon	14.95
Start and Run a Profitable Consulting Business	12.95
Start and Run a Profitable Craft Business	10.95
Start and Run a Profitable Restaurant	10.95
Start and Run a Profitable Retail Business	11.95
Starting a Successful Business in Canada	12.95
Step-Parent Adoptions	12.95
Taking Care	7.95
Upper Left-Hand Corner	10.95
Working Couples	5.50
Write Right!	5.50

PROVINCIAL TITLES

Divorce Guide
❑ B.C. 9.95 ❑ Alberta 9.95 ❑ Saskatchewan 12.95
❑ Manitoba 11.95 ❑ Ontario 12.95

Employer/Employee Rights
❑ B.C. 7.95 ❑ Alberta 6.95 ❑ Ontario 6.95

Incorporation Guide
❑ B.C. 14.95 ❑ Alberta 14.95 ❑ Manitoba/Saskatchewan 12.95 ❑ Ontario 14.95

Landlord/Tenant Rights
❑ B.C. 7.95 ❑ Alberta 6.95 ❑ Ontario 7.95

Marriage & Family Law
❑ B.C. 7.95 ❑ Alberta 8.95 ❑ Ontario 7.95

Probate Guide
❑ B.C. 12.95 ❑ Alberta 10.95 ❑ Ontario 11.95

Real Estate Guide
❑ B.C. 8.95 ❑ Alberta 7.95 ❑ Ontario 8.50

Small Claims Court Guide
❑ B.C. 7.95 ❑ Alberta 7.50 ❑ Ontario 7.50

Wills
❑ B.C. 6.50 ❑ Alberta 6.50 ❑ Ontario 5.95
❑ Wills/Probate Procedure for Manitoba/Saskatchewan 5.95

PACKAGED FORMS

Divorce Forms
❑ B.C 11.95 ❑ Alberta 10.95 ❑ Saskatchewan 12.95
❑ Manitoba 10.95 ❑ Ontario 14.95

Incorporation
❑ B.C 12.95 ❑ Alberta 14.95 ❑ Saskatchewan 14.95
❑ Manitoba 14.95 ❑ Ontario 14.95 ❑ Federal 7.95
❑ Minute Books 17.95
❑ Power of Attorney Kit 9.95

Probate
❑ B.C. Administration 14.95 ❑ B.C. Probate 14.95
❑ Alberta 14.95 ❑ Ontario 15.50

❑ Rental Form Kit (B.C., Alberta, Saskatchewan, Ontario) 4.95

❑ Have You Made Your Will? 5.95

❑ If You Love Me Put It In Writing – Contract Kit 14.95

❑ If You Leave Me Put It In Writing – B.C. Separation Agreement Kit 14.95

Interim Agreement
❑ B.C. 2.50 ❑ Alberta 2.50 ❑ Ontario 2.50

Note: All prices subject to change without notice.

Books are available in book and department stores, or use the order form below. Please enclose cheque or money order (plus sales tax where applicable) or give us your MasterCard or Visa number (please include validation and expiry dates).

(PLEASE PRINT)

Name _____

Address _____

City _____ Province _____

Postal Code _____

❑ Visa/ ❑ MasterCard Number_____

Validation Date_____ Expiry Date _____

If order is under $20.00, add $1.00 for postage and handling.
Please send orders to:
SELF-COUNSEL PRESS
1481 Charlotte Road
North Vancouver, British Columbia   V7J 1H1

❑ Check here for free catalogue.

SELF-COUNSEL PRESS INC..
AMERICAN
ORDER FORM

11/88

NATIONAL TITLES

_____	Abbreviations & Acronyms	5.95
_____	Arrested! Now What?	7.95
_____	Asking Questions	7.95
_____	Assertiveness for Managers	9.95
_____	Basic Accounting	5.95
_____	Be a Better Manager	8.95
_____	Between the Sexes	8.95
_____	Business Etiquette Today	7.95
_____	Business Guide to Effective Speaking	6.95
_____	Business Guide to Profitable Customer Relations	7.95
_____	Business Writing Workbook	9.95
_____	Buying and Selling a Small Business	
_____	Death in the Family	8.95
_____	Design Your Own Logo	9.95
_____	Entrepreneur's Self-Assessment Guide	9.95
_____	Exporting From the United States	12.95
_____	Family Ties That Bind	7.95
_____	Financial Control for the Small Business	5.50
_____	Financial Freedom on $5 a Day	7.95
_____	Franchising in the U.S	5.95
_____	Fundraising for Non-profit Groups	5.50
_____	How You Too Can Make a Million in the Mail Order Business (Washington & Oregon)	9.95
_____	Immigrating to Canada	14.95
_____	Immigrating to the U.S.A.	14.95
_____	Keyboarding for Kids	7.95
_____	Learn to Type Fast	11.50
_____	Managing Stress	7.95
_____	Marketing Your Product	12.95
_____	Marketing Your Service	12.95
_____	Mobile Retirement Handbook	9.95
_____	Newcomer's Guide to the U.S.A.	12.95
_____	Parent's Guide to Day Care	5.95
_____	Parent's Guide to Understanding Teenagers and Suicide	8.95
_____	Photography & The Law	7.95
_____	Planning for Financial Independence	11.95
_____	Practical Guide to Financial Management	6.95
_____	Practical Time Management	6.95
_____	Radio Documentary Handbook	8.95
_____	Ready-to-Use Business Forms	9.95
_____	Selling Strategies for Service Businesses	12.95
_____	Small Business Guide to Employee Selection	6.95
_____	Start and Run a Profitable Beauty Salon	14.95
_____	Start and Run a Profitable Consulting Business	12.95
_____	Start and Run a Profitable Craft Business	10.95
_____	Start and Run a Profitable Restaurant	10.95
_____	Start and Run a Profitable Retail Business	11.95
_____	Starting a Successful Business on the West Coast	12.95
_____	Taking Care	7.95
_____	Upper Left-Hand Corner	10.95
_____	Working Couples	5.50

STATE TITLES — WASHINGTON AND OREGON

Please indicate which state edition is required

_____ Divorce Guide
❏ Washington (with forms) 14.95 ❏ Oregon 11.95

_____ Employer/Employee Rights
❏ Washington 5.50

_____ Incorporation and Business Guide
❏ Washington 12.95 ❏ Oregon 12.95

_____ Landlord/Tenant Rights
❏ Washington 6.95 ❏ Oregon 9.95

_____ Marriage & Family Law
❏ Washington 8.95 ❏ Oregon 4.95

_____ Probate Guide
❏ Washington 9.95

_____ Real Estate Buying/Selling Guide
❏ Washington 6.95 ❏ Oregon 3.95

_____ Small Claims Court Guide
❏ Washington 4.50

_____ Wills
❏ Washington 6.95 ❏ Oregon 6.95

PACKAGED FORMS

_____ Divorce
❏ Oregon Set A (Petitioner) 14.95
❏ Oregon Set B (Co-petitioners) 12.95

_____ If You Love Me — Put It In Writing 7.95

_____ Incorporation
❏ Washington 12.95 Oregon 12.95

_____ Probate
❏ Washington 9.95

_____ Rental Form Kit 3.95

_____ Will and Estate Planning Kit 595

All prices subject to change without notice.

Check here for free catalog ❏

(PLEASE PRINT)

NAME_____

ADDRESS _____

CITY _____

STATE _____

ZIP CODE _____

Check or money order enclosed _____
*If order is under $20, add $1.50 for postage and handling
Washington residents add 8.1% sales tax.*
Please send orders to:

SELF-COUNSEL PRESS INC.
1303 N. Northgate Way
Seattle, Washington, 98133